DREAMING WAR

ALSO BY GORE VIDAL

NOVELS

Williwaw
In a Yellow Wood
The City and the Pillar
The Season of Comfort
A Search for the King
Dark Green, Bright Red
The Judgment of Paris
Messiah
Julian
Washington, D.C.
Myra Breckinridge
Two Sisters
Burr
Myron
1876
Kalki
Creation
Duluth
Lincoln
Myra Breckinridge and Myron
Empire
Hollywood
Live from Golgotha
The Smithsonian Institution
The Golden Age

GORE VIDAL

DREAMING

WAR

Blood for Oil and the Cheney-Bush Junta

Thunder's Mouth Press / Nation Books
New York

Dreaming War:
Blood for Oil and the Cheney-Bush Junta

Copyright © 2002 by Gore Vidal

Published by
Thunder's Mouth Press / Nation Books
161 William St., 16th Floor
New York, NY 10038

Nation Books is a co-publishing venture of the Nation Institute and
Avalon Publishing Group Incorporated.

*How We Missed the Saturday Dance; The Last Empire; In the Lair of the
Octopus; With Extreme Prejudice; The Union of the State; Mickey Mouse,
Historian; Democratic Vistas; Three Lies to Rule By;* and *Japanese Intentions
in the Second World War* from *The Last Empire* by Gore Vidal, copyright
© 2001 by Gore Vidal. Used by permission of Doubleday, a division of
Random House.

*The Last Defender of the American Republic: An Interview with Gore
Vidal.* Used by permission of Marc Cooper © 2002.

Library of Congress Cataloging-in-Publication Data is available.

ISBN 1-56025-502-1

9 8 7 6 5 4 3 2 1

Book design by Sue Canavan
Printed in the United States of America
Distributed by Publishers Group West

Contents

III.

NOTE

The late and great comedienne Hermione Gingold once said of her long life's journey: "It would appear that I have tried everything except incest and folk dancing."

As I look back on fifty-six years of writing, I seem to have used most literary forms available to me except journalism. I started, at twenty, with a novel; and went on to record, among other things, the history of the United States from revolution to millennium. Now I have returned—or rather, turned to the oldest form of American political discourse, the pamphlet. And so I dedicate *Dreaming War* to Publius, the joint authors of The Federalists, in whose words our republic truly began.

—GORE VIDAL

November 2002

I

DEMOCRATIC VISTAS

The Vice President to Richard Nixon and bribe-taker to many, Spiro Agnew, was once inspired to say, "The United States, for all its faults, is still the greatest nation in the country." Today, even in the wake of the Supreme Court's purloining of the election for the forty-third President, Spiro must be standing tall among his fellow shades. Have we not come through, yet again? As we did in 1888, when Grover Cleveland's plurality of the popular vote was canceled by the intricacies of the Electoral College, and as we even more famously did in 1876, when the Democrat Samuel Tilden got 264,000 more votes than the Republican Rutherford B. Hayes, whose party then challenged the votes in Oregon, South Carolina, Louisiana and—yes, that slattern Florida. An electoral commission chosen by Congress gave the election to the loser, Hayes, by a single vote, the result of chicanery involving a bent Supreme Court Justice appointed by the sainted Lincoln.

3

Revolution was mooted but Tilden retired to private life and to the pleasures of what old-time New Yorkers used to recall, wistfully, as one of the greatest collections of pornography in the Gramercy Park area of Manhattan.

Until December 12, we enjoyed a number of quietly corrupt elections, decently kept from public view. But the current Supreme Court, in devil-may-care mood, let all sorts of cats out of its bag—such as a total commitment to what the far right euphemistically calls family values. Justice Antonin Scalia—both name and visage reminiscent of a Puccini villain—affirmed family values by not recusing himself from the Bush–Gore case even though his son works for the same law firm that represented Bush before the Court. Meanwhile, Justice Clarence Thomas's wife works for a far-right think tank, the Heritage Foundation, and even as her husband attended gravely to arguments, she was vetting candidates for office in the Bush administration.

Elsewhere, George W. Bush, son of a failed Republican President, was entrusting his endangered Florida vote to the state's governor, his brother Jeb.

On the other side of family values, the Gore clan has, at times, controlled as many as a half-dozen Southern legislatures. They are also known for their forensic skill, wit, learning—family characteristics the Vice President modestly kept under wraps for fear of frightening the folks at large.

American politics is essentially a family affair, as are most oligarchies. When the father of the Constitution, James Madison, was asked how on earth any business could get done in Congress when the country contained 100 million people whose representatives would number half a thousand, Madison took the line that oligarchy's iron law always obtains: A few people invariably run the show; and keep it, if they can, in the family.

Finally, those founders, to whom we like to advert, had such a fear and loathing of democracy that they invented the Electoral College so that the popular voice of the people could be throttled, much as the Supreme Court throttled the Floridians on December 12. We were to be neither a democracy, subject to majoritarian tyranny, nor a dictatorship, subject to Caesarean folly.

Another cat let out of the bag is the Supreme Court's dedication to the 1 percent that own the country. Justice Sandra Day O'Connor couldn't for the life of her see why anyone would find the Palm Beach butterfly ballot puzzling. The subtext here was, as it is so often with us, race. More votes were invalidated by aged Votomatic machines in black districts than in white. This made crucial the uncounted ten thousand Miami-Dade ballots that recorded no presidential vote. Hence the speed with which the Bush campaign, loyally aided and abetted by a 5-to-4 majority of the Supreme Court, invented a series of delays to keep those votes from ever being counted because, if they were, Gore would have won the election. Indeed he did win the election until the Court, through ever-more-brazen stays and remands, with an eye on that clock ever ticking, delayed matters until, practically speaking, in the eyes of the five, if not all of the four, there was no longer time to count, object of an exercise that had sent trucks filled with a million ballots from one dusty Florida city to the next, to be kept uncounted.

During this slow-paced comedy, there was one riveting moment of truth that will remain with us long after G. W. Bush has joined the lengthening line of twilight Presidents in limbo. On the Wednesday before the Thursday when we gave thanks for being the nation once hailed as the greatest by Agnew, the canvassing board in Dade County was, on the orders of the Florida Supreme Court, again counting ballots when an organized crowd stormed into the county building, intimidating the counters and refusing to give their names to officials. The *Miami Herald*, a respectable paper, after examining various voting trends, etc., concluded that Gore had actually carried Florida by twenty-three thousand votes. The *Herald* plans to examine those much-traveled ballots under Florida's "sunshine" law. I suspect that the ballots and their chads will be found missing.

Thanksgiving came and went. The ballots toured up and down the Florida freeways. Gore was accused of trying to steal an election that he had won. The black population was now aware that, yet again, it had not been taken into account. There had been riots. Under Florida law, anyone with a criminal record—having been convicted of a felony—loses all civil rights. Thousands of blacks were so accused and denied the vote; yet most so listed were not felons or were guilty only of misdemeanors. In any case, the calculated delays persuaded two of the four dissenting judges that there was no time left to count.

Justice John Paul Stevens, a conservative whose principal interest seems to be conserving our constitutional liberties rather than the privileges of corporate America, noted in his dissent: "One thing, however, is certain. Although we may never know with complete certainty the identity of the winner of this year's presidential election, the identity of the loser is perfectly clear. It is the nation's confidence in the judge as an impartial guardian of the rule of law."

What will the next four years bring? With luck, total gridlock. The two houses of Congress are evenly split. Presidential adventurism will be at a minimum. With bad luck (and adventures), Chancellor Cheney will rule. A former Secretary of Defense, he has said that too little money now goes to the Pentagon even though last year it received 51 percent of the discretionary budget. Expect a small war or two in order to keep military appropriations flowing. There will also be tax relief for the very rich. But bad scenario or good scenario, we shall see very little of the charmingly simian George W. Bush. The military—Cheney, Powell, et al.—will be calling the tune, and the whole nation will be on constant alert, for, James Baker has already warned us, Terrorism is everywhere on the march. We cannot be too vigilant. Welcome to Asunción. Yes! We have no bananas.

The Nation
January 8/15, 2001

Goat Song:
Unanswered Questions —
Before, During, After 9/11

O n August 24, 1814, things looked very dark for freedom's land. That was the day the British captured Washington, D.C., and set fire to the Capitol and White House. President Madison took refuge in the nearby Virginia woods, where he waited patiently for the notoriously short attention span of the Brits to kick in, which it did. They moved on and what might have been a Day of Utter Darkness turned out to be something of a bonanza for the D.C. building trades and upmarket realtors.

One hundred and eighty-seven years later—and one year after 9/11, we still don't know by whom we were struck that Tuesday, or for what true purpose. But it is does seem fairly plain to many civil libertarians that 9/11 put paid not only to our fragile Bill of Rights, but also to our once-envied republican system of government which had abruptly taken a mortal blow the previous year, when the Supreme

Court did a little dance in 5-4 time and replaced an elected president with the oil-and-gas Cheney-Bush junta.

Of course, for some years, it has been no secret that Corporate America openly and generously pays for our presidential elections (Bush-Gore in 2000 cost them $3 billion); they also own the Media, which is kept well-nourished by disinformation from executive-controlled secret agencies like the CIA. Media also daily assures us that since we are the most envied and admired people on earth, everyone else on earth is eager to immigrate to the U.S. so that he can share in the greatest pie ever baked by arbitragers. Meanwhile, our more and more unaccountable government is pursuing all sorts of games around the world that we the spear carriers (formerly the people) will never learn of. Even so, in the last year, with help from foreign friends, we are getting some answers to the question: Why weren't we warned in advance of 9/11? Apparently, we were warned, repeatedly; for the better part of a year, we were told that there would be unfriendly visitors to our skies sometime in September '01, but the Cheney-Bush junta neither informed us nor protected us despite Mayday warnings from Presidents Putin and Mubarak, from Mossad, and even from elements of our long-suffering FBI. A joint panel of Congressional intelligence committees is currently reporting (September 19, 2002, *New York Times*) that as early as 1996, Pakistani terrorist Abdul Hakim Murad confessed to federal agents that he was "learning to fly an aircraft in order to crash a plane into CIA HQ."

Only CIA Director George Tenet seemed to take the various threats seriously. In December '98, he issued "a declaration of war." So impressed was the FBI by his warnings that as of September 10, 2001, "the FBI still had only one analyst assigned full time to al Qa'eda."

From a briefing prepared for the junta at the beginning of July 2001: "Based on a review of all sources reporting over the last five months, we believe that UBL will launch a significant terrorist attack against U.S. and/or Israeli interests in the coming weeks. The attack will be spectacular and designed to inflict mass casualties against U.S. facilities or interests. Attack preparations have been made. Attack will occur with little or no warning." And so it came to pass; yet, the National Security Advisor says she never suspected that hijackings meant anything but the kidnapping of planes.

Happily, somewhere over the Beltway, there is Europe— recently declared anti-Semitic by the junta's Media because most of Europe wants no war with Iraq and the junta does for reasons we may now begin to understand, thanks to European and Asian investigators with their relatively free media.

On the subject "How and Why America Was Attacked September 11, 2001," the best, most balanced report, thus far, is by Nafeez Mosaddeq Ahmed. . . . Yes, yes, I know he is one of Them. But they often know things that we don't—particularly about what *we* are up to. A political scientist, Ahmed is executive director of the Institute for Policy Research & Development, "a think tank dedicated to the promotion of human rights, justice and peace" in Brighton, England. The book, *The War on Freedom,* has just been published in the USA by a small but reputable homeland publisher.

Ahmed provides a background for our ongoing war against Afghanistan, a view that in no way coincides with what the junta has told us. He has drawn on many sources, most tellingly on American whistle-blowers who are beginning to come forth and bear witness—like those FBI agents who warned their superiors that al Qa'eda was planning a kamikaze strike against New York and Washington, only to be told that if they went public with these warnings, they would suffer under the National Security Act. Lately, several of these agents have engaged David P. Schippers, chief investigative counsel for the House Judiciary Committee, to represent them in court *if* he is not elsewhere. As many Americans will recall, the majestic Schippers managed the successful impeachment of President Clinton in the House of Representatives. He may, if the Iraqi adventure should go wrong, be obliged to perform the same high service for George W. Bush—the junta's cheerleader—who allowed the American people to go unwarned about an imminent attack upon two of our cities in anticipation of a planned strike by the United States against the Taliban in Afghanistan.

The *Guardian* (UK, September 26, 2001) reported that in July 2001, pre–9/11, a group of interested parties met in a Berlin hotel to listen to a former State Department official, Lee Coldren, as he passed on a message from the Bush administration that ". . . the United States was so disgusted with the Taliban that they might be considering some military action . . . the chilling quality of this private warning was that it came—according to one of those present, the Pakistani diplomat Niaz Naik—accompanied by specific details of how Bush would succeed. . . . " Four days earlier, the *Guardian* had reported that "Osama bin Laden and the Taliban received threats of possible American military strikes against them two months before the terrorist assaults on New York and Washington . . . [which] raises the possibility that bin Laden . . . was launching a pre-emptive strike in response to what he saw as US threats." A replay of the "day of infamy" in the Pacific sixty-two years earlier?

Two days *before* September 11, Bush was presented with

a draft of a National Security Presidential Directive out-
lining a global campaign of military, diplomatic and intelligence action targeting al Qa'eda, buttressed by the threat
of war. According to NBC News: "President Bush was
expected to sign detailed plans for a worldwide war against
al Qa'eda . . . but did not have the chance before the terrorist attacks. . . ." The directive, as described to NBC News,
was essentially the same war plan as the one put into action
after September 11. "The administration most likely was
able to respond so quickly . . . because it simply had to pull
the plans 'off the shelf.'"

Finally, BBC News, September 18, 2001: "Niaz Naik, a
former Pakistan Foreign Secretary, was told by senior American officials in mid-July that military action against
Afghanistan would go ahead by the middle of October." It
was Naik's view that Washington would not drop its war for
Afghanistan even if bin Laden were to be surrendered
immediately by the Taliban."

Was Afghanistan then turned to rubble in order to
avenge the three thousand Americans slaughtered by
Osama? Hardly. The junta is convinced that Americans are
so simple minded that they can deal with no scenario
more complex than the venerable lone, crazed killer (this
time with zombie helpers) who does evil just for the fun of
it 'cause he hates us, 'cause we're rich 'n' free 'n' he's not.

The unlovely Osama was chosen on aesthetic grounds to be the frightening logo for our long contemplated invasion and conquest of Afghanistan, planning for which had been "contingency" some years before 9/11 and, again, from December 20, 2000, when Clinton's outgoing team devised a plan to strike at Osama and al Qa'eda in retaliation for their assault on the battleship *Cole*. Clinton's National Security Advisor, Sandy Berger, personally briefed his successor, Condoleezza Rice, on the plan, but the lady, still very much in her role as a director of Chevron-Texaco, with special duties regarding Pakistan and Uzbekistan, now denies, in the best junta tradition, any briefing by her predecessor in the most important federal job that has to do with the nation's security. A year and a half later (August 12, 2002), fearless *Time* magazine reported this odd memory lapse.

Osama, if it was he and not a nation, simply provided the necessary shock to put in train a war of conquest. But conquest of what? What is there in dismal dry sandy Afghanistan worth conquering? Zbigniew Brzezinski tells us exactly what in a 1997 Council on Foreign Relations study called *The Grand Chessboard: American Primacy and Its Geostrategic Imperatives*.

The Polish-born Brzezinski was the hawkish National Security Advisor to President Carter. In *The Grand Chessboard,*

Brzezinski gives a little history lesson. "Ever since the continents started interacting politically, some five hundred years ago, Eurasia has been the center of world power." Eurasia is all the territory east of Germany. This means Russia, the Mideast, China, and parts of India. Brzezinski acknowledges that Russia and China, bordering oil-rich central Asia, are the two main powers threatening American hegemony in that area.

He takes it for granted that the U.S. must exert control over the former soviet republics of Central Asia, known to those who love them as "the Stans": Turkmenistan, Uzbekistan, Tajikstan, and Kyrgyzstan, all "of importance from the standpoint of security and historical ambitions to at least three of their most immediate and most powerful neighbors—Russia, Turkey and Iran, with China signaling." Brzezinski notes how the world's energy consumption keeps increasing; hence, who controls Caspian oil/gas will control the world economy. Brzezinski then, reflexively, goes into the standard American rationalization for empire. We want nothing, ever, for ourselves, only to keep bad people from getting good things with which to hurt good people. "It follows that America's primary interest is to help ensure that no single [other] power comes to control this geopolitical space and that the global community has unhindered financial and economic access to it."

Brzezinski is quite aware that American leaders are wonderfully ignorant of history and geography so he really lays it on, stopping just short of invoking politically incorrect "manifest destiny." He reminds the Council just how big Eurasia is: 75 percent of the world's population is Eurasian. If I've done the math right, that means we've only got control, to date, of a mere 25 percent of the world's folks. More! "Eurasia accounts for 60% of the world's GNP and three-fourths of the world's known energy resources."

Brzezinski's master plan for "our" globe has obviously been accepted by the Cheney-Bush junta. Corporate America, long overexcited by Eurasian mineral wealth, has been aboard from the beginning.

Ahmed sums up: "Brzezinski clearly envisaged that the establishment, consolidation and expansion of US military hegemony over Eurasia through Central Asia would require the unprecedented, open-ended militarization of foreign policy, coupled with an unprecedented manufacture of domestic support and consensus on this militarization campaign."

Afghanistan is the gateway to all these riches. Will we fight to seize them? It should never be forgotten that the American people did *not* want to fight in either of the twentieth century's world wars but President Wilson maneuvered us into World War I while President Roosevelt maneuvered the Japanese into striking the first blow at Pearl Harbor, causing us to enter World War II as the result of a massive external attack. Brzezinski understands all this and, in 1997, he is thinking ahead: "Moreover, as America becomes an increasingly multi-cultural society, it may find it more difficult to fashion a consensus on foreign policy issues, except in the circumstance of a truly massive and widely perceived direct external threat." Thus was the gun produced that belched black smoke over Manhattan and the Pentagon.

Since the Iran-Iraq wars of the '80s and early '90s, Islam has been demonized as a Satanic terrorist cult that encourages suicide attacks—contrary, it should be noted, to the Islamic religion. Osama has been portrayed accurately, it would seem, as an Islamic zealot. In order to bring this evildoer to justice (dead or alive) Afghanistan, the object of the exercise, was made safe not only for democracy, but for Union Oil of California, whose proposed pipeline, from Turkmenistan to Afghanistan to Pakistan and the Indian Ocean port of Karachi, had been abandoned under the Taliban's chaotic regime. Currently, the pipeline is a go-project thanks to the junta's installation of a Unocal employee as American envoy to the newly born democracy whose president is also a former Unocal employee.

Once Afghanistan looked to be within the fold, the

junta, which had managed with some success to pull off a complex diplomatic-military caper, abruptly replaced Osama, the personification of evil, with Saddam Hussein. This has been hard to explain since there is nothing to connect Iraq with 9/11. Happily, "evidence" is now being invented. But it's uphill work, not helped by stories in the U.S. press about the vast oil wealth of Iraq itself, which must—for the sake of the free world—be reassigned to U.S. and European consortiums.

As Brzezinski foretold, "a truly massive and widely perceived direct external threat" made it possible for the junta's cheerleader president to dance a war dance before Congress. *"A long war!"* he shouted with glee. Then he named an incoherent Axis of Evil to be fought. Although Congress did not give him the FDR special—a declaration of war—he did get permission to go after Osama, who may now be skulking in Iraq.

Post–9/11, American media was filled with preemptory denunciations of unpatriotic "conspiracy theorists," who not only are always with us, but are usually easy for media to discredit since it is an article of faith that there are no conspiracies in American life. Yet, a year or so ago, who would have thought that most of Corporate America had been conspiring with accountants to cook their books since—well, at least the bright dawn of the age of Reagan and deregulation. Ironically, less than a year after the massive danger from without, we were confronted with an even greater enemy from within: Golden Calf capitalism. Transparency? One fears that greater transparency will only reveal armies of maggots at work beneath the skin of a culture that needs a bit of a lie-down in order to collect itself before taking its next giant step, which is to conquer Eurasia, a potentially fatal adventure not only for our frazzled institutions but for us the presently living.

Complicity. The behavior of President George W. Bush on 9/11 certainly gives rise to all sorts of suspicions. I can think of no other modern chief of state who would continue to pose for "warm" pictures of himself listening to a young girl telling stories about her pet goat while hijacked planes were slamming into three famous buildings.

Constitutionally, Bush is not only chief of state, he is commander-in-chief of the armed forces. Normally, a commander in such a crisis would go straight to headquarters and direct operations while receiving the latest intelligence as to who, where, what.

This is what Bush actually did—or did not do—according to Stan Goff, a retired twenty-six-year U.S. Army veteran who has taught Military Science and Doctrine at West Point. Goff writes ("The So-called Evidence is a Farce"): "I have no idea why people aren't asking some very specific questions about the actions of Bush and company on the day of the attacks. Four planes get hijacked and deviate from their flight plan, all the while on FAA radar." Incidentally, Goff, like the other astonished military experts, cannot fathom why the government's automatic "standard order of procedure in the event of a hijacking" was not followed. Once a plane has deviated from its flight plan, fighter planes are sent up to find out why. That is mandatory law and does not require presidential approval, which only needs to be given if there is a decision to shoot down the plane. Goff spells it out:

> The planes are all hijacked between 7:45 and 8:10 AM Eastern Daylight Time. Who is notified? This is an event already that is unprecedented. But the President is not notified and going to a Florida elementary school to hear children read.
>
> By around 8:15 AM it should be very apparent that something is terribly wrong. The President is glad-handing teachers. By 8:45, when American Airlines' Flight 11 crashes into the World Trade Center, Bush is settling in with children for his photo ops at Booker Elementary. Four planes have obviously been hijacked simultaneously, an event never before seen in history, and one has just dived into the world's best-known twin towers, and still no one notifies the nominal Commander-in-Chief.
>
> No one has apparently scrambled [sent aloft] any Air Force interceptors either. At 9:03, United Flight 175 crashes into the remaining World Trade Center building. At 9:05 Andrew Card, the Presidential Chief-of-Staff, whispers to George

W. Bush [who] "briefly turns somber" according to reporters. Does he cancel the school visit and convene an emergency meeting? No. He resumes listening to second graders . . . and continues the banality even as American Airlines' Flight 77 conducts an unscheduled point turn over Ohio and heads in the direction of Washington DC.

Has he instructed Chief-of-Staff Card to scramble the Air Force? No. An excruciating 25 minutes later, he finally deigns to give a public statement telling the United States what they have already figured out—that there's been an attack by hijacked planes on the World Trade Center. There's a hijacked plane beelining to Washington, but has the Air Force been scrambled to defend anything yet? No.

At 9:30 when he makes his announcement, American Flight 77 is still ten minutes from its target, the Pentagon. The Administration will later claim they had no way of knowing that the Pentagon might be a target, and they thought Flight 77 was headed to the White House, but the fact is that the plane has already flown South and past the White House no-fly zone, and is in fact tearing through the sky at 400 nauts.

At 9:35, this plane conducts another turn, 360 degrees over the Pentagon, all the while being tracked by radar, and the Pentagon is not evacuated, and there are still no fast-movers from the Air Force in the sky over Alexandria and DC. Now the real kicker: a pilot they want us to believe was trained at a Florida puddle-jumper school for Piper Cubs and Cessnas, conducts a well-controlled downward spiral descending the last 7000 feet in two-and-a-half minutes, brings the plane in so low and flat that it clips the electrical wires across the street from the Pentagon, and flies it with pinpoint accuracy into the side of the building at 460 nauts.

When the theory about learning to fly this well at the puddle-jumper school began to lose ground, it was added that they received further training on a flight simulator. This is like saying you prepared your teenager for her first drive on I-40 at rush hour by buying her a video driving game. . . . There is a story being constructed about these events.

There is indeed, and the more it is added to the darker it becomes. The nonchalance of General Richard B. Myers, acting Joint Chief-of-Staff, is as puzzling as the president's campaigning-as-usual act. Myers was at the Capitol chatting with Senator Max Cleland. A sergeant, writing later in the AFPS (American Forces Press Service), describes Myers at the Capitol. "While in an outer office, he said, he saw a television report that a plane had hit the World Trade Center. 'They thought it was a small plane or something like that,' Myers said. So the two men went ahead with the office call."

Whatever Myers and Cleland had to say to each other (more funds for the military?) must have been riveting because, during their chat, the AFPS reports, "The second World Trade Center tower was hit by another jet. 'Nobody informed us of that,' Myers said. 'But when we came out, that was obvious. Then, right at that time, somebody said the Pentagon had been hit.' " Finally, somebody—another body?—"thrust a cell phone in Myers' hand" and, as if by magic, the commanding general of NORAD—our Airspace Command—was on the line just as the hijackers' mission had been successfully completed except for the failed one in Pennsylvania. In later testimony to the Senate Armed Forces Committee, Myers says that he thinks that, as of his cell phone talk with NORAD, "the decision was at that point to start launching aircraft."

This statement would have been quite enough in our old

serious army/air force to launch a number of courts-martial with an impeachment or two thrown in. First, Myers claims to be uninformed until the third strike. But the Pentagon had been overseeing the hijacked planes from at least the strike at the first tower. But not until the third strike at the Pentagon was the decision made to get the fighter planes up. Finally, this one is the dog that did not bark. According to law, the fighters should have been up around 8:15. If they had, all three hijacked planes might have been shot down. I don't think Sergeant Stan Goff is being unduly picky when he wonders who and what kept the Air Force from following its normal procedure instead of waiting an hour and twenty minutes until the damage was done and only then launching the fighters. Obviously, somebody had ordered the Air Force to make no move to intercept those hijackings until . . . what?

A wistful note is sounded by the commander of the Russian air force, Anatoli Kornukov. He concedes that they have had similar situations, but "as soon as something like that happens here, I am reported [to] right away and in a minute we are all up." One wonders if he wonders that if the U.S. is so ill-defended, why the old Soviet Union didn't risk a tiny sneak attack? Meanwhile, it is rumored that Putin has offered to help us defend ourselves in the future.

January 28, '02. The Canadian media analyst Barry Zwicker summed up on CBC-TV:

> Throughout the northeastern United States are many air bases. But that morning no intercep-tors responded in a timely fashion to the highest alert situation. This includes the Andrews squadrons which have the longest lead-time and are twelve miles from the White House. What-ever the explanation for the huge failure, there have been no reports, to my knowledge, of rep-rimands. This further weakens the "Incompe-tence Theory." Incompetence usually earns reprimands. This causes me to ask—if there were "stand down" orders.

A year later, BBC (August 29, 2002) reports on 9/11 that "there are only four fighters on ready status in the north-eastern U.S." Conspiracy? Coincidence? Error?

It is interesting how often in our history, when disaster strikes, incompetence is considered a better alibi than . . . well, yes, there are worse things. After Pearl Harbor, Con-gress moved to find out why Hawaii's two military com-manders, General Short and Admiral Kimmel, had not anticipated the Japanese attack. But President Roosevelt preempted that investigation with one of his own. Short and Kimmel were broken for incompetence. The "truth" is still obscured to this day.

But Pearl Harbor has been much studied over the years. 9/11, it is plain, is never going to be investigated if our secretive junta has anything to say about it. At the end of January '02, CNN reported:

> President Bush personally asked Senate Majority Leader Tom Daschle Tuesday to limit the Congressional investigation into the events of September 11, Congressional and White House sources told CNN. . . . The request was made at a private meeting with Congressional leaders. . . . Sources said Bush initiated the conversation. . . . He asked that only the House and Senate intelligence committees look into the potential breakdowns among federal agencies that could have allowed the terrorist attacks to occur, rather than a broader inquiry that some lawmakers have proposed. . . . Tuesday's discussion followed a rare call from Vice President Dick Cheney last Friday to make the same request . . ."

The excuse given, according to Daschle, was that an investigation "would take resources and personnel away" from the war on terrorism in the event of a wider inquiry that is not limited to the assumption that the administration's inaction was solely a consequence of "breakdowns among federal agencies." So for reasons that we must never know, those "breakdowns" are to be the goat. That they were more likely to be not break but "stand-downs" is not for us to pry. Certainly, the hour-twenty-minute failure to put fighter planes in the air could not have been due to a break-down throughout the entire Air Force along the East Coast. Mandatory standard operating procedure had been told to cease and desist.

Meanwhile, Media was assigned its familiar task of inciting public opinion against Osama bin Laden, still not the proven mastermind. These media blitzes often resemble the magician's classic gesture of distraction: as you watch the rippling bright colors of his silk handker-chief in one hand, he is planting the rabbit in your pocket with the other. We were quickly assured that Osama's enor-mous family with its enormous wealth had broken with him, as had the royal family of his native Saudi Arabia. The CIA swore, hand on heart, that Osama had not worked for them in the war against the Soviet occupation of Afghanistan. Finally, the rumor that the Bush family had in any way profited by its long involvement with the bin

Laden family was—what else?—simply partisan bad taste. But Bush Junior's involvement with evil goes back at least to 1979 when his first failed attempt to become a player in the big Texas oil league brought him together with one James Bath of Houston, a family friend, who gave Bush Jr. $50,000 for a 5 percent stake in Bush's firm Arbusto (Spanish for "shrub"). At this time, according to Wayne Madsen (*In These Times*, November 12, 2001), Bath was:

> the sole US business representative for Salem bin Laden, head of the wealthy Saudi Arabian family and a brother (one of 17) to Osama bin Laden. . . . In a statement issued shortly after the September 11 attacks, the White House vehemently denied the connection, insisting that Bath invested his own money, not Salem bin Laden's, in Arbusto. In conflicting statements, Bush at first denied ever knowing Bath, then acknowledged his stake in Arbusto and that he was aware Bath represented Saudi interests . . . after several reincarnations, Arbusto emerged in 1986 as Harken Energy Corporation. When Harken ran into trouble, a year later, Saudi Sheikh Abdullah Taha Bakhsh . . .

Bush Jr., like Bush Sr. has, in times of financial distress, often depended upon the kindness of burnooses—or is it burniece?

Back of the junior Bush is the senior Bush, gainfully employed by the Carlyle Group, which has ownership in at least 164 companies worldwide, inspiring admiration in that staunch friend to the wealthy, the *Wall Street Journal*, who noted, as early as September 27, '01:

> If the US boosts defense spending in its quest to stop Osama bin Laden's alleged terrorist activities, there may be one unexpected beneficiary: Mr. bin Laden's family . . . the well-heeled Saudi Arabia clan . . . is an investor in a fund established by Carlyle Group, a well-connected Washington merchant bank specializing in buyouts of defense and aerospace companies. . . . Osama is one of more than 50 children of Mohammed bin Laden who built the family's $5 billion business.

The *Wall Street Journal* might have suggested that another beneficiary of the war in Afghanistan would be, as *Judicial Watch* put it (September 28, 2001), "George H. W. Bush, the father of President Bush, works for the bin Laden family business in Saudi Arabia through the Carlyle Group, an international consulting firm. The senior Bush had met with the bin Laden family at least twice." *Judicial Watch* Chairman and General Counsel Larry Klayman breaks through this gray narrative of corporate greed at a time of peril for the U.S.: "The idea of the President's father, an ex-president himself, doing business with a company under investigation by the FBI in the terror attacks of September 11 is horrible."

But Bush *pere et fils*, in pursuit of wealth and office, is beyond shame or, one cannot help but think, good sense. There is evidence that they are blocking investigation of the bin Laden connection with terrorism. *Agence France Presse* writes, November 7, 2001: "FBI agents in the United States probing relatives of Saudi-born terror suspect Osama . . . were told to back off soon after George W. Bush became president . . ." Apparently, "two other U.S.-based members of the bin Laden family are suspected to have links with a possible terrorist organization." Yet, according to BBC-TV's *Newsnight* (November 6, 2001), ". . . just days after the hijackers took off from Boston aiming for the Twin Towers, a special charter flight out of the same airport whisked 11 members of Osama's family off to Saudi Arabia. That did not concern the White House. Their official line is that the bin Ladens are above suspicion." *Above the Law* (Green Press, February, 2002) sums up; ". . . we had what looked like the biggest failure of the intelligence community since

Pearl Harbor but what we are learning now is it wasn't a failure, it was a directive." True? False? Bush Junior will be under oath during the impeachment interrogation. Will we hear "What is a directive? What is *is*?"

Although the U.S. had, for some years, fingered Osama as a mastermind terrorist who had blown up a couple of our embassies in Africa and put a hole in the side of a destroyer berthed in Yemen, no serious attempt had been made pre–9/11 to "bring him to justice dead or alive, innocent or guilty," as Texan law of the jungle requires. Clinton's plan to act was given Condoleezza Rice by Sandy Berger, you will recall, but she says she does not.

As far back as March 1996, when Osama was in Sudan, Major General Elfatih Erwa, Sudanese Minister for Defense, offered to extradite him. According to the *Washington Post* October 3, 2001; " . . . The Sudanese security services, he [Erwa] said, would happily keep close watch on bin Laden for the United States. But if that would not suffice, the government was prepared to place him in custody and hand him over. . . . [US officials] said, 'Just ask him to leave the country. Just don't let him go to Somalia,' " where he had once been given credit for the successful al Qa'eda attack on American forces in '93 that killed eighteen Rangers. "Erwa said in an interview, 'We said he will go to Afghanistan, and they [U.S. officials] said, "Let him." ' "

In 1996 Sudan expelled Osama and three thousand of his associates. Two years later, the Clinton administration, in the great American tradition of never having to say thank you for Sudan's offer to hand over Osama, proceeded to missile-attack Sudan's Al Shifa's pharmaceutical factory on the ground that Sudan was harboring bin Laden terrorists who were making chemical and biological weapons when they were simply making vaccines for the UN.

Four years later, John O'Neill, a much-admired FBI agent, was reported to have "complained bitterly that the US State Department—and behind it the oil lobby who make up President Bush's entourage—blocked attempts to prove bin Laden's guilt. The US ambassador to Yemen forbade O'Neill (and his FBI team) . . . from entering Yemen in August 2001. O'Neill resigned in frustration and took on a new job as head of security at the World Trade Center. He died in the September 11 attack . . ." (*Irish Times,* November 19, 2001). Obviously, Osama has enjoyed bipartisan American support since his enlistment in the CIA's war to drive the Soviets out of Afghanistan. But by 9/11 there was no Soviet occupation of Afghanistan; indeed, there was no Soviet Union.

I watched Bush and Cheney on CNN when the Axis of Evil speech was given and the "long war" proclaimed. Iraq, Iran, North Korea were fingered immediately as enemies to be clobbered because they might or might not be harboring terrorists who might or might not destroy us in the night. So we must strike first whenever it pleases us. "Odd," said a fellow veteran of World War II, "that Bush and Cheney are so delighted to put us at war when, during Vietnam, they were both what we used to call draft dodgers." But then we agreed that in our politics the sissies are always cheerleading the real guys on to go give their lives. Real soldiers like Colin Powell are less gung ho. Thus, we declared war on terrorism—an abstract noun which cannot be a war at all, as you need a country for that. Of course, there was innocent Afghanistan, which was leveled from a great height, but then what's collateral damage—like an entire country—when you're targeting the personification of all evil according to *Time* and the *New York Times* and the networks, et cetera?

As it proved, the conquest of Afghanistan had nothing to do with Osama. He was simply a pretext for replacing the Taliban with a relatively stable government that would allow Union Oil of California to lay its pipeline for the profit of, among others, the Cheney-Bush junta.

Background? All right. The headquarters of Unocal are, as might be expected, in Texas. In December 1997, Taliban representatives were invited to Sugarland, Texas. At that time, Unocal had already begun training Afghan men in the skills required for pipeline construction, with U.S. government approval. BBC News, December 4, 1997:

> A spokesman for the company, Unocal, said the Taliban were expected to spend several days at the company's [Texas] headquarters . . . a BBC regional correspondent says the proposal to build a pipeline across Afghanistan is part of an international scramble to profit from developing the rich energy resources of the Caspian Sea. . . . Nearly 140 people were enrolled last month in Kandahar. . . .

The Inter Press Service (IPS), reported, "Some Western business interests are warming up to the Taliban despite the movement's" institutionalization of terror, massacres, abductions and impoverishment. CNN, October 8, 1996: "The United States wants good ties [with the Taliban] but can't openly seek them while women are severely oppressed." The Taliban, rather better organized than rumored, hired for PR one Laili Helms, a niece of Richard Helms, former director of the CIA.

In October 1996, the German *Frankfurter Rundschau* reported that Unocal "has been given the go-ahead from the new holders of power in Kabul to build a pipeline from Turkmenistan via Afghanistan to Pakistan. It would lead from Krasnovodsk on the Caspian Sea to Karachi on the Indian Ocean coast."

This was a real coup for Unocal, as well as other candidates for pipelines, including Condoleezza's old employer, Chevron. Although the Taliban was already notorious for its imaginative crimes against the human race, the *Wall Street Journal*, May 23, 1997, scenting big bucks, fearlessly announced, "Like them or not, the Taliban are the players most capable of achieving peace in Afghanistan at this moment in its history."

The *New York Times*, May 26, 1997, leaped aboard the pipeline juggernaut. "The Clinton Administration has taken the view that a Taliban victory would . . . act as counterweight to Iran . . . and would offer the possibility of new trade routes that could weaken Russian and Iranian influence on the region."

But by 1999, it was clear that the Taliban could never provide us the security we would need to protect our fragile pipelines. The arrival of Osama as warrior for Allah on the scene refocused, as it were, the bidding. New alliances were now being made. Frederick Starr of Johns Hopkins wrote in the *Washington Post* December 19, 2000: ". . . the United States has quietly begun to align itself with those in the Russian government calling for military action against Afghanistan and has toyed with the idea of a new raid to wipe out Osama bin Laden." That was December. Then the Bush administration bought the idea of an invasion of Afghanistan (inspired by Sandy Berger?). Then came September and October . . . Unocal, *nous voilà!*

An unexpected joy of this abstract war has been the emergence of our elfin Defense Secretary Rumsfeld as a major TV comic. Since the Gulf War, we are now used to seeing foreign correspondents report, not from the field but huddled together in a briefing room at the Pentagon while, in this case, Rumsfeld works them over in front of the camera. He has a number of grins and grimaces that trigger instant laughter. His looks register: Amazement—I thought I'd heard everything. As you know, *I* cannot answer that.

You know that—head shakes in sorrow. Will they never learn—shoulders heave. Highly selective, self-serving sound bites are served up and the correspondents are as in the dark as the rest of us about the war. Thanks to Europe—where bluebirds fly—some news gets back from the front. Also, there is *USA Today,* November 11, 2001, "The US combat commander in Afghanistan said Thursday that apprehending Osama bin Laden isn't one of the missions of *Operation Enduring Storm.*"

Out the window go all those demonizing stories. One's first instinct is that the field commander's job is now at risk. We've fought too many wars with no clearly defined enemy for no specific objective to indulge in another. But, no, the scenario has simply been switched from Evil Personified to "We have not *said* that Osama bin Laden is a target of this effort." General Franks told reporters at his first Pentagon briefing since the war began: "What we are about," he said, "is the destruction of the al Qa'eda network as well as the . . . Taliban that provide harbor to bin Laden and al Qa'eda."

A helpful aide chimed in, "If tomorrow morning someone told us Osama's dead, that doesn't mean we're through in Afghanistan." Although with much fanfare we went forth to wreak our vengeance on the crazed sadistic religious zealot who slaughtered three thousand American citizens, once that "war" was under way, Osama was dropped as irrelevant and so we're back to the Unocal pipeline, now a go-project. In the light of what we know today, it is unlikely that the Junta was ever going to capture Osama *alive:* he has tales to tell. One of Rumsfeld's best numbers now is: "Where is he? Somewhere? Here? There? Somewhere? Who knows?" And we get his best twinkle. He must also be delighted—and amazed—that the Media has bought the absurd story that Osama, if alive, would still be in Afghanistan, underground, waiting to be flushed out instead of in a comfortable mansion in Osama-loving Jakarta, two thousand miles to the east and easily accessible by Flying Carpet One.

Many commentators of a certain age have noted how Hitlerian our Junta sounds as it threatens first one country for harboring terrorists and then another. It is true that Hitler liked to pretend to be the injured—or threatened—party before he struck. But he had many great predecessors not least Imperial Rome. Stephen Gowans' *War in Afghanistan: A $28 Billion Racket* quotes Joseph Schumpteter, who in 1919,

> described ancient Rome in a way that sounds
> eerily like the United States in 2001: "There was
> no corner of the known world where some

interest was not alleged to be in danger or under
actual attack. If the interests were not Roman,
they were those of Rome's allies; and if Rome
had no allies, the allies would be invented. . . .
The fight was always invested with an aura of
legality. Rome was always being attacked by evil-
minded neighbors."

We have only outdone the Romans in turning metaphors
like the war on terrorism, or poverty, or AIDS into actual
wars on targets we appear, often, to pick at random in order
to maintain turbulence in foreign lands.

As of August 1, 2002, trial balloons were going up all over
Washington, D.C., to get world opinion used to the idea that
"Bush of Afghanistan" had gained a title as mighty as his
father's "Bush of the Persian Gulf" and Junior was now eager
to add Iraq-Babylon to his diadem. These various balloons
fell upon Europe and the Arab world like so many lead
weights. But something new has been added since the classic
Roman Hitlerian mantra: "They are threatening us; we must
attack first." Now everyone is more or less out in the open.
The International Herald Tribune (August 1, 2002) wrote:

The leaks began in earnest July 5, when the *New
York Times* described a tentative Pentagon plan that

it said called for an invasion by a US force of up to 250,000 that would attack Iraq from the north, south and west. On July 10, the *Times* said that Jordan might be used as a base for the invasion.

The Washington Post reported, July 28, that "many senior US military officers contend that President Saddam Hussein poses no immediate threat. . . . "

And the status quo should be maintained. Incidentally, this is the sort of debate that the founding fathers intended the Congress, not military bureaucrats, to conduct in the name of we the people. But that sort of debate has, for a long time, been denied us.

One refreshing note is now being struck in a fashion unthinkable in Imperial Rome: the cheerful admission that we habitually resort to provocation: "Defense Secretary Donald Rumsfeld has threatened jail to anyone found to have been behind the leaks. But a retired army general, Fred Woerner, tends to see a method behind the leaks. 'We may already be executing a plan,' he said recently. 'Are we involved in a preliminary psychological dimension of causing Iraq to do something to justify a US attack or make concessions? Somebody knows.' " That is plain.

Elsewhere in this interesting edition of the *Herald Tribune* wise William Pfaff (too wise and too principled to obtain a New York outlet) writes:

> A second Washington debate is whether to make an unprovoked attack on Iran to destroy a nuclear power reactor being built there with Russian assistance, under inspection by the International Atomic Energy Agency, within the terms of the Nuclear Nonproliferation Treaty of which Iran is a signatory. . . . No other government in the world would support such an action, other than Israel's [which] would do so not because it expected to be attacked by Iran but because it, not unreasonably, opposes any nuclear capacity in the hands of any Islamic government.

> Of all the enemies to public liberty, war is, perhaps, the most to be dreaded because it comprises and develops the germ of every other. As the parent of armies, war encourages debts and taxes, the known instruments for bringing the many under the domination of the few. In war, too, the discretionary power of the executive is extended . . . and all the means of seducing the minds, are added to those of subduing the force, of the people. . . .

Thus, James Madison warned us at the dawn of our republic.

Post–9/11, thanks to the "domination of the few," Congress and Media are silent as the executive, through propaganda and skewed polls, seduces the public mind while heretofore unthinkable centers of power like Homeland Defense are being constructed and 4 percent of the country has recently been invited to join TIPS, a civilian spy system to report on anyone who look suspicious—or who objects to what the executive is doing at home or abroad.

Although every nation knows how—if it has the means and the will—to protect itself from thugs of the sort that brought us 9/11, war is not an option. Wars are for nations, not rootless gangs. You put a price on their heads and hunt them down. In recent years, Italy has been doing that with the Sicilian Mafia—and no one has yet suggested bombing Palermo.

But the Cheney-Bush junta wants a war in order to dominate Afghanistan, build a pipeline, gain control of the oil of the Eurasian Stans for their business associates as well as to do as much damage to Iraq and Iran on the ground that one day those evil countries may carpet our fields of amber grain with anthrax or something.

The Media, never much good at analysis, is more and more breathless and incoherent. On CNN, even the stolid Jim Clancy started to hyperventilate when an Indian academic tried to explain how Iraq was once our ally and "friend" in its war against our Satanic enemy, Iran. "None of that conspiracy stuff," snarled Clancy. Apparently, "conspiracy stuff" is now shorthand for unspeakable truth.

As of August, at least among economists, a consensus was growing that, considering our vast national debt (we borrow $2 billion a day to keep the government going) and a tax base seriously reduced by the junta in order to benefit the 1 percent who own most of the national wealth, there is no way that we could ever find the billions needed to destroy Iraq in "a long war" or even a short one, with most of Europe lined up against us. Germany and Japan paid for the Gulf War, reluctantly—with Japan, at the last moment, irritably quarreling over the exchange rate at the time of the contract. Now Germany's Schroeder says no. Japan is mute.

But the tom-toms keep beating revenge and the fact that most of the world is opposed to our war seems only to bring hectic roses to the cheeks of Bush Senior of the Carlyle Group, Bush Junior of Harken, Cheney of Halliburton, Condoleezza Rice of Chevron-Texaco, Rumsfeld of Occidental, Gale Norton of BP Amoco. If ever there was an administration that should recuse itself in matters dealing with energy, it is the current junta. But they are unlike any other administration in our history. Their hearts are plainly elsewhere, making money, far from our mock Roman temples, while, alas, we are left only with their heads, dreaming of war, preferably against weak peripheral states.

Mohammed Heikal is a brilliant Egyptian journalist-observer, and sometime foreign minister. On October 10, 2001, he said to the *Guardian:*

Bin Laden does not have the capabilities for an

operation of this magnitude. When I hear Bush talking about al Qa'eda as if it was Nazi Germany or the Communist Party of the Soviet Union, I laugh because I know what is there. Bin Laden has been under surveillance for years: every telephone call was monitored and al Qa'eda has been penetrated by American intelligence, Pakistani intelligence, Saudi intelligence, Egyptian intelligence. They could not have kept secret an operation that required such a degree of organization and sophistication.

The former president of Germany's domestic intelligence service, Eckehardt Werthebach (*American Free Press* of December 4, 2001), spells it out. The 9/11 attack required "years of planning," while the scale of the attacks indicates that they were a product of "state-organized actions." There it is. Perhaps, after all, Bush Junior was right to call it a war. But which *state* attacked us?

Will the suspects please line up. Saudi Arabia? "No, no. Why, we are paying you $50 million a year for training the royal bodyguard on our own holy if arid soil. True, the kingdom contains many wealthy well-educated enemies but . . . . " Bush Senior and Junior exchange a knowing look. Egypt? No way. Dead broke despite U.S. baksheesh. Syria? No funds. Iran? Too proud to bother with a parvenu state like the U.S. Israel? Sharon is capable of anything. But he lacks the guts and the grace of the true Kamikaze. Anyway, Sharon was not in charge when this operation began with the planting of "sleepers" around the U.S. flight schools five or six years ago. The United States? Elements of Corporate America are eager not only for "a massive external attack" that would make it possible for us to go to war whenever the president sees fit while suspending civil liberties. (The 342 pages of the USA Patriot Act were plainly prepared before 9/11.)

Bush Senior and Junior are giggling now. Why? Because Clinton was president back then. As the former president leaves the line of suspects, he says, more in anger than in sorrow, "When we left the White House we had a plan for an all-out war on al Qa'eda. We turned it over to this administration and they did nothing. Why?" Biting his lip, he goes on. The Bushes no longer giggle. Pakistan breaks down. "I did it! I confess! I couldn't help myself. Save me. I am an evildoer."

Apparently, Pakistan did do it—or some of it. We must now go back to 1979, when "the largest covert operation in the history of the CIA" was launched in response to the Soviet invasion of Afghanistan. Central Asia specialist Ahmed Rashid wrote (*Foreign Affairs,* November-December 1999):

With the active encouragement of the CIA and

Pakistan's ISI [Inter Services Intelligence] who
wanted to turn the Afghan jihad into a global
war, waged by all Muslim states against the
Soviet Union, some 35,000 Muslim radicals,
from 40 Islamic countries joined Afghanistan's
fight between 1982 and '92 . . . more than
100,000 foreign Muslim radicals were directly
influenced by the Afghan jihad.

The CIA covertly trained and sponsored these warriors.

In March 1985, President Reagan issued National Security Decision Directive 166, increasing military aid while
CIA specialists met with the ISI counterparts near
Rawalpindi, Pakistan. *Jane's Defense Weekly* (September 14,
2001) gives the best overview: "The trainers were mainly
from Pakistan's Inter Services Intelligence (ISI) agency who
learnt their craft from American Green Beret commandos
and Navy Seals in various US training establishments." This
explains the reluctance of the administration to explain
why so many unqualified persons, over so long a time, got
visas to visit our hospitable shores. While in Pakistan,
"Mass training of Afghan mujahideen [zealots] was subse-
quently conducted by the Pakistan army under the super-
vision of the elite Special Services. . . . In 1988, with US
knowledge, bin Laden created al Qa'eda (The Base), a con-

glomerate of quasi-independent Islamic terrorist cells in countries spread across at least 26 or so countries. . . . Washington turned a blind eye to al Qa'eda."

September 4, 2001, London's *Daily Telegraph* reported that the Director General of the ISI, General Mahmoud Ahmed, arrived in Washington. On September 10, the Pakistani daily, *The News,* remarked how

> ISI Chief Mahmoud's week-long presence in Washington has triggered speculation about the agenda of his mysterious meetings at the Pentagon and National Security Council. . . . Officially, State Department sources say he is on a routine visit in return to CIA Director George Tenet's earlier visit to Islamabad. Official sources confirm that he met Tenet this week.

No further details were given. But then, on October 8, Mahmoud was dismissed as Director of the ISI and took early retirement. The *Times* of India (September 8, 2001) was the first in the field with the reason:

> Top sources here confirmed on Tuesday, that the general lost his job because of the "evidence" India produced to show his links to one of the suicide

bombers that wrecked the World Trade Center. The
US authorities sought his removal after confirming
the fact that $100,000 were wired to hijacker
Mohammed Atta from Pakistan by Ahmad Uhmar
Sheikh at the instance of General Mahmoud.

Mohammed Atta is now known to have been in command of
the nineteen men who hijacked the four planes on September
11, 2001. He died in the first tower collision. Why did General
Mahmoud, during his visit to Washington, send him money?

Certainly, this is one of those questions that will be
asked during the coming impeachment trial of George W.
Bush, Jr. Let us hope that Chief Cheney has explained the
Pakistan connection to him.

When Mohammed Atta's plane struck the World Trade
Center, Bush and the child at the Florida elementary school
were discussing her goat. By coincidence, our word "tragedy"
comes from the Greek: for "goat" *tragos* plus *oide* for "song."
"Goat-song." It is highly suitable that this lament, sung in
ancient satyr plays, should have been heard again at the
exact moment when we were struck by fire from heaven, and
a tragedy whose end is nowhere in sight began for us.

October 2002

MENANDERING TOWARD
ARMAGEDDON

Louis Menand is Distinguished Professor of English at City University of New York Graduate Center. He writes a sort of cultural column for *The New Yorker*, which means he is a neoconservative, since the magazine's cultural editor would allow no other in a slot once renowned for its occupancy by Edmund Wilson. Characteristically, Menand deals entirely in received opinion, which he gently re-tales in a dim run-on sort of style that can best be described as menandering. He is given to broad assertions; then, faced with a sudden dead-end, he . . . well, menanders. One has the sense that without editorial direction, he is essentially apolitical, but since 9/11 and the responses of what he calls most "cultural and political critics," it seems he does have opinions to share because "It just proves what I've always said [to Mrs. Menand?], the attacks were treated as geopolitics for dummies." But how

could they *not* be dummies, considering a public educational system that no longer teaches geography in primary
schools, much less comparative history or even relevant
American history.

The half dozen or so "critics" that he quotes "are," he
notes contentedly, "so devoid of surprise as to be almost
devoid of thought." Well, thanks to our educational system
and a Media that reports only good news from Corporate
America, anyone trying to make sense of why we were
recently struck by Moslem zealots will need to have the
wheel reinvented for him. This takes a lot of marshaling of
the obvious. Like what is a Moslem? But even here Menand
is in a bit of a bind. No neo-con wants the *reason* for the
attack to be analyzed too carefully because, sooner or later,
we must always go back to the U.S.-Israeli connection, an
absolutely taboo subject in our Media not to mention political life. Easier to say that anyone who even suggests that
U.S. activities might have brought on the attack is simply
an "America-hater" or (lower voice) anti-Semite or worse—
as if *anything* is worse. Since Menand is quite aware of the
low quality of our political discourse in this matter, he
shifts the 9/11 attack from a deliberate attack by angry parties (which seems obvious to most of us and worthy of
analysis) to, of all things, an "accident." Some accident! To
paraphrase Winston Churchill.

Once Menand had done his magic trick, he can say how "disappointing to be told in the books published so far on the 'meaning' of September 11th, what we have always been told about ourselves." Idle menandering, now becomes filibustering: "People who walk away from a car crash in which they might have died . . . sometimes react by assessing their entire lives—as though the accident were a judgment. It wasn't, it was an accident." To translate 9/11 as a random car-crash is sublime idiocy of the sort that only an American neo-con, protecting a "secret," would dare menander.

Our schoolteacher next approaches his principal targets, Noam Chomsky and me. He takes his place in front of the blackboard. Visualize that Manhattan classroom. Lecture hall? I sense an American flag to the professor's far right. Is there a Graduate Center flag? Furled? A bit of throat clearing. Deep breath; exhale; "Anti-Americanism is the view that the United States is basically a global bad guy" (twinkle in the eye on "bad"—say it ain't so!), "A nation that was founded on the impulses of materialism and expansionism, and that is getting more materialistic and expansionist every decade." Chuckle? Raised eyebrow? Homeland Security is watching you, Professor. Stronger voice now: nitty-gritty is on the table. "This (pause) school of thought needs to be distinguished from what might be

called dissenting patriotism, which is the view that the
United States is basically a virtuous republic that has
recently been betrayed by runaway corporate capitalism
and by the emergence of a national security state contemptuous of individual liberties and international law. Noam
Chomsky belongs to the first school."

And, according to the professor, I belong to the second.
Unfortunately, he has carefully, with the adverb "recently"
distorted my position. What has happened to our never-
virtuous but always-evolving toward (the Founders had
hoped) true republican virtue, has been implicit from the
beginning, and the current evils of Corporate America and
the National Security State are hardly recent. In fact,
anyone who believes that all this is a mere development of
the last fifty years is historically naïve, a case the menander
would like—clumsily, if I may say so—to make in my case,
even though I, not he, am the historian here. But, Hark!
Let's see what he means to do with America-hater Noam.

Menand:

> Chomsky does not suggest that September 11
> attacks were a legitimate response to American
> aggression. His point is only that it is naïve to
> imagine that the United States is an innocent
> victim. In fact, Chomsky unequivocally con-

demns the attacks, and bin Laden and his network, and this leaves him with the problem of
explaining the causal relevance of the bombing
of Al-Shifa (apparently the result of an intelligence failure) and the Iraqi deaths (a claim
based on disputed statistics) to the massacres at
the Pentagon and World Trade Center. Here he
has recourse to the highly useful concept of
"blowback."

This is a paradigm of high-gear menandering, particularly
the late point of departure, the bombing of the notorious
aspirin factory by Clinton as the trigger for 9/11, quite for-
getting that the true genesis was the founding of the current state of Israel, midwifed by Harry Truman in '48
followed by the later occupations and annexations of Pales-
tinian land in what was, according to Zionist zealots, either
empty land or luxury housing moodily abandoned by
wealthy Arabs, like the Said family, as they withdrew to
their winter quarters at Cairo's Shepheard's Hotel.

Menand is careful to say that Chomsky is not gloating
over 9/11, but he has a "problem" establishing a causal link
between Clinton's idle bombing of that aspirin (actually,
vaccine) factory in Sudan and 9/11. Apparently, Chomsky,
stymied, can only invoke "blowback." Well, anything in

the matter of Israel's colonial aggression in Palestine is bound to carry with it some—if not a great deal—of blowback. This is where the menandering style can be useful. Acknowledging no history at all in the Middle East pre–Clinton's strike, damage can be well and truly controlled. Tit for tat, as they say in neo-con land.

But Menander intuits that he isn't quite making his case against Chomsky the Moralist. Compulsively, he now makes the first of several false analogies. "Blowback, as the term is used in the literature on September 11, is intended to carry moral weight!" Here it comes: "If you insist on trampling through other people's flower gardens, you can't complain when you get stung is the general idea." So far, so good. "But this is true, without moral implication of any sufficiently complex undertaking."

Surely, three thousand dead provide more than a considerable sufficiency. Perhaps the adjective "complex" is the key. But where one can fret over the degree of moral complexity in Hardy's *A Pair of Blue Eyes,* one cannot use the same calipers to measure the forces that caused the rain of fire from heaven upon us which, defined by death, brought a great and complex and reverberating moral weight to bear. Menander is now edgily searching for a better analog. "It is like saying, if you keep building huge passenger ships, sooner or later one of them is going to hit an iceberg. . . . "

False analogy. Start again. He does. The new point of departure is the Afghan resistance movement of 1979 rather than Israel's partial conquest of Palestine in 1949. Self-rattled, he connects 9/11 causally with the Soviet failed conquest of Afghanistan. He sternly challenges those who say 9/11 was a wake-up call. "Wake up to what?" he cries, still pretending not to get it. Then he menanders: "The fact that the United States is involved in the affairs of other nations?" We have always been involved. He plods on. "If that is a problem, we are left with only two alternatives: isolationism or conquest." Suicide or murder? Has it come to this? Only two? And who says so? Ah, Professor Menand, I believe. Well, we shall see if he enlists as a sharpshooter in the Cheney-Bush army that will be sent into Iraq, Iran, wherever oil bubbles in the sand.

Then he gets to me. Briefly, as they say every five seconds on CNN news shows, "Gore Vidal is a dissenting patriot, a nostalgist of the lost republic." But, first, like so many contemporary English teachers, Menand obsesses with the sales of writers who write. Chomsky's *9/11* became a best-seller . . . "a more interesting fact than the book itself which consists of transcripts of interviews, given mostly to *foreign* journalists." The "foreign" hurts, or does it? Actually, Chomsky is largely blacked out by U.S. media, and so he has only foreign interviewers—and his books and numerous readers.

As for me, "The only reasonable conclusion to be drawn from the success of *Perpetual War* . . . a paperback best-seller, is that if you put Gore Vidal's name on the cover people will buy it." *Magari,* as the Italians say ("would that it were so"). Professor Menand's problem is that although he is no doubt some sort of scholar, he is not used to reading anything that might contradict what he thinks he already knows. What Chomsky and I have in common is an interest in public matters and a fascination with the lies that power tells us, lies we deconstruct, lies which also fascinate—and affect—a number of our countrymen who do read seriously. There's nothing much more to it than that.

The schoolteacher counts the pages in which I deal with 9/11, only 18 out of 160. He is baffled that I give "a twenty-page chart of United States Military Operations, on loan from an outfit called the Federation of American Scientists." That chart is the reason, dear professor, why people bought the book. Were you ever to write honestly, let us say, of the havoc Israel has wrought in the Moslem world, you, too, will be viewed as an honest messenger. The some two hundred recorded military unilateral strikes that the U.S. has made against Second and Third World countries is a great scandal not discussed in our Media or known to our taxpayers. Your reference to the Federation of American Scientists as a sort of shady anonymous "outfit" is calculated to suggest some sort of conspiracy. For the record, the federation was founded in 1945 by a group of atomic scientists at Los Alamos. They were concerned about the implications of atomic weapons in particular, of science in general vis-à-vis the matter of human survival. Of their current board of sponsors, I counted some forty-five Nobel laureates in science. Some outfit.

The Distinguished Professor affects not to understand why I included my piece on McVeigh and the American "Patriot/Militia" movements "as there is no cogent connection" between McVeigh and bin Laden. "Cogent" is a tired schoolteacher word seldom used by actual writers who are compelled to cogency by nature. If there were not a compelling reason for me to juxtapose a homegrown revolutionary movement against a government seen to them to be alien and punitive and external enemies provoked by that government, I would not have put them together. Most Americans do get the point: others, of course, may be gazing elsewhere.

Finally, he does boldly link me with Chomsky as an "America-hater." This is on a par with those Nazis who, aware that Thomas Mann hated Hitler, declared that he hated Germany, a very different thing. I cannot think that anyone will ever take seriously the likes of the Menanderer on American patriotism. That others hate, demonstratively,

America, we saw on 9/11. I try to give some reasons for their anger. Incidentally, I did not record any of the CIA's activities, like the overthrowing of governments in Guatemala, Iran, Chile, Nicaragua, Haiti, etc. Also, I would never conflate a truly bad—even evil—administration like that of Cheney-Bush with America, a complex of peoples whose republic was largely replaced by the National Security State in 1950 in favor of perpetual war and then, as of Election 2000, the presidency ceased to be within the traditional gift of We the People. Chomsky and I do not hate America, which, after all, is us, too. Or was. We are also not eccentric. The junta at Washington is.

November 2002

II

Three Lies to Rule By

In the end, the American presidential campaign of 2000 ostensibly (pre-fraud) came down to a matter of Character. Specifically, to the characters of two male citizens of hitherto no particular interest to the polity. But then personality is about all that our media can cope with, since the American political system, despite ever more expensive elections, sees to it that nothing of an overtly political nature may be discussed. It is true that one candidate, daringly, if briefly, suggested that since 1 percent of the population owns most of the country, as well as quite a bit of the globe elsewhere, perhaps that 1 percent ought not to pay even less tax than it currently does. This tore it. For a moment, the red flag snapped in CNN's early light, but by twilight's last gleaming, that banner was struck, and no real issue was touched on again.

What then is a real issue? Currently, the United States spends twenty-two times as much as our potential enemies (the seven designated rogue states of concern) spend combined. It used to be that true politics involved an accounting of where the people's tax money goes and why. Since the American military currently gets over half of each year's federal revenue, that should have been the most important subject to chat about. But not this year, and so, dutifully, each candidate pledged himself to ever greater spending for the Great War Machine, as it idly trawls about the globe in search of enemies, leaving us with nothing to chatter about except Character. With *moral* character. Or, as Dr. Elaine May once put it so well: "I like a moral problem so much better than a real problem."

Although one candidate was immediately perceived to be something of a dope—and dyslexic to boot (defense: it's not *his* fault, so why are you picking on him?), there are, we were sternly told, worse things in a President. Like what? *Like lying*. When this bunch of garlic was hoisted high, a shudder went through us peasants in our Transylvanian villages as we heard, across haunted moors, the sound of great leathern wings. The undead were aloft.

One candidate was deemed a liar because he exaggerated. He never actually said that he alone had invented the Internet, but he implied that he might have had more to do with its early inception than he had. Worse, he said that his mother-in-law's medicine cost more than his dog's

identical medicine, when he had—I've already forgotten
which—either no mother-in-law or no dog. By now the
Republic was reeling. The vileness of it all! Could we entrust
so false a figure to hold in his hand war's arrows, peace's
laurel? All in all, the $2 billion to $3 billion that the election cost the generous 1 percent through its corporate paymasters was, by all reckoning, the most profoundly
irrelevant in a political history which seems determined to
make a monkey of Darwin while exalting the creationist
point of view, Manichaean version.

Today's sermon is from Montaigne: "Lying is an
accursed vice. It is only our words which bind us together
and make us human. If we realized the horror and weight
of lying, we would see that it is more worthy of the stake
than other crimes. . . . Once let the tongue acquire the
habit of lying and it is astonishing how impossible it is to
make it give it up."

But our subject is not the people, those quadrennial
spear-carriers, but the two paladins, one of whom will
presently be entrusted with the terrible swift nuclear sword,
thus becoming the greatest goodest nation that ever was
robustly incarnate.

"We are a nation based on Truth," the Republican managers of the impeachment of sex-fibber President Clinton
constantly reminded us, unaware that his constituents

were, perversely, rallying round him. Pleased, no doubt, by the metaphysics of his "What is *is*?" After all, what is truth, as a Roman bureaucrat once rather absently put it. Yet . . .

"Yet" is the nicest of words in English when logically, nonpregnantly used. The American global empire rests on a number of breathtaking presidential lies that our court historians seldom dare question. It would seem that the Hitler team got it about right when it comes to human credulity: the greater the lie, the more apt it is to be believed. The price of the perhaps nonexistent dog's medicine is not going to go unchallenged, but President Franklin Delano Roosevelt's deliberate provocation of the Japanese, in order to force them into attacking us and thus bring us into the Second World War, is simply not admissible. Contemporary journalism's first law, "What ought not to be true is not true," is swiftly backed up by those who write the "history" stories to be used in schools. Happily, I have lived long enough to indulge in the four most beautiful words in the English language: "I told you so."

In *Burr* (1973), I relit, as it were, the image of that demonized figure, Aaron Burr. In passing, I duly noted that his chief demonizer, the admirable-in-most-things, save a tendency toward hypocrisy, Thomas Jefferson, had lived connubially with a slave girl, Sally Hemings, by whom he had a number of children, kept on as slaves. Dumas Malone, the leading Jefferson biographer of the day, denounced my portrait of Jefferson as "subversive," because, as he put it, no gentleman could have had sexual relations with a slave and, since Mr. Jefferson was the greatest gentleman of that era, he could not have . . . On such false syllogisms are national myths set. Recent testing shows that many of Hemings's descendants contain the golden DNA of Jefferson himself. Loyalists say that it was an idiot nephew who fathered Sally's children. How? Since Jefferson and Sally lived pretty much as man and wife at Monticello, the idea of the nephew, banjo in hand, making his way up the hill to the house, time and again, to get laid by Jefferson's companion boggles the mind. So much for a great lie that court historians and other propagandists insist that Americans believe. Why is it so grimly important? Since the relationship between black and white is still the most delicate of subjects for Americans, Jefferson must be marble-pure and so outside his own great formulation and invitation to the peoples of all the world: the pursuit of happiness.

That was yesterday. Today, any scrutiny of the three powerful myths which Americans and their helpers in other lands are obliged to accept will set off fire alarms. In *The*

Golden Age (largely covering the years 1940–50 as viewed from Washington, D.C., by our rulers), I make three cases involving presidential whoppers. One, Franklin Delano Roosevelt (whose domestic policies—the New Deal—I admire) deliberately provoked the Japanese into attacking us at Pearl Harbor. Why? As of 1940, he wanted us in the war against Hitler, but 80 percent of the American people wanted no European war of any kind after the disappointments of 1917. He could do nothing to budge an isolationist electorate. Luckily for him (and perhaps the world), Japan had a military agreement with Germany and Italy. For several years, Japan had been engaged in an imperial mission to conquer China. Secretly, FDR began a series of provocations to goad the Japanese into what turned out to be an attack on our fleet at Pearl Harbor, thus making inevitable our prompt, wholehearted entry into the Second World War. There is a vast literature on this subject, beginning as early as 1941 with Charles A. Beard's *President Roosevelt and the Coming of War* and continuing to the current *Day of Deceit* by Robert B. Stinnett, now being argued about in the U.S. Stinnett gives the most detailed account of the steps toward war initiated by FDR, including the November 26, 1941, ultimatum to Japan, ordering them out of China while insisting they renounce their pact with the Axis powers; this left Japan with no alternative but war, the object of the exercise.

The second great myth was that Harry Truman, FDR's successor, dropped his two atom bombs on Hiroshima and Nagasaki because he feared that a million American lives would be lost in an invasion (that was the lie he told at the time). Admiral Nimitz, on the spot in the Pacific, and General Eisenhower, brooding elsewhere, disagreed: the Japanese had already lost the war, they said. No nuclear bombs, no invasion was needed; besides, the Japanese had been trying to surrender since the May 1945 devastation of Tokyo by U.S. B-29 bombers.

The third great myth was that the Soviets began the Cold War because, driven by the power-mad would-be world conqueror, Stalin, they divided Germany, forcing us to create the West German republic, and then, when Stalin viciously denied us access to our section of Berlin (still under four-power rule as determined at Yalta), we defied him with an airlift. He backed down, foiled in his invasion of France, his crossing of the Atlantic, and so on.

These are three very great myths which most historians of the period knew to be myths, but which court historians, particularly those with salaries that are paid by universities with federal grants for research and development, either play down or flatly deny.

David Hume tells us that the Many are kept in order by the Few through Opinion. The *New York Times* in the U.S. is the Opinion-maker of the Few for some of the Many; so when the paper draws the line, as it were, other papers in other lands take heed and toe it. In *The Golden Age*, I revealed, tactfully I thought, life in Washington during the decade from the fall of France to Pearl Harbor to the Cold War and Korea. No one needs to know any history at all to follow the story. Even so, one American reviewer was upset that I did not know how "dumbed-down" (his phrase) Americans were, and how dare I mention people that they had never heard of, such as Harry Hopkins?

But I am a fairly experienced narrator, and each character is, painlessly I hope, explained in context. Unfortunately, the new pop wisdom is that you must only write about what the readers already know about, which, in this case at least, would be an untrue story.

The *New York Times* hired a British journalist, once associated with the *New Republic*, a far-right paper unfavorable to me (it is a propagandist for Israel's Likudite faction, much as the *Washington Times* supports the line of its proprietor, Korea's Dr. Sun Moon). The hired journalist knew nothing of the period I was writing about. He quotes an aria from Herbert Hoover which he thinks I made up, when, as always with the historical figures that I quote, I only record what they are said to have said.

Hoover regarded, rightly or wrongly, FDR as in the same totalitarian mold as he saw Hitler, Mussolini, and Stalin: "You cannot extend the mastery of the government over the daily working life of a people without at the same time making it the master of the people's souls and thoughts." Our best modern historian, William Appleman Williams, in *Some Presidents: Wilson to Nixon* (1972), noted that it was Hoover's intuition that, in the first third of the twentieth century, the virus of totalitarian government was abroad in the world, and that Hitler in his demonic way and Stalin in his deadly bureaucratic way and FDR in his relatively melioristic way were each responding to a common Zeitgeist.

For a right-wing hired hand this should have been a profound analysis, but the reviewer fails to grasp it. He also ignores Hoover's astonishing aside: "What this country needs is a great poem." Most damaging to the integrity of my narrative (and the historians I relied on), the reviewer declares, without evidence, that . . . But let me quote from a letter by the historian Kai Bird, which, to my amazement, the *New York Times* published (usually they suppress anything too critical of themselves or their Opinion-makers):

Twice the reviewer dismisses as "silly" Vidal's assertion that Harry Truman's use of the atomic bomb on Hiroshima was unnecessary because Japan had been trying for some months to surrender.

Such assertions are neither silly nor . . . a product of Vidal's "cranky politics." Rather Vidal has cleverly drawn on a rich and scholarly literature published in the last decade to remind his readers that much of what orthodox court historians have written about the Cold War was simply wrong. With regard to Hiroshima, perhaps Vidal had in mind Truman's July 18, 1945, handwritten diary reference to a "telegram from Jap emperor asking for peace."

Or this August 3, 1945, item from the diary of Walter Brown:

Brown notes a meeting with Secretary of State James F. Byrnes, Admiral W. D. Leahy, and Truman at which all three agreed, "Japs looking for peace." . . . But Truman wanted to drop the bomb; and did. Why? To frighten Stalin, a suitable enemy for the U.S. as it was about to metamorphose from an untidy republic into a

national security state at "perpetual war," in
Charles A. Beard's phrase, "for perpetual peace."

I fear that the *TLS* review of *The Golden Age* battened on
the inaccuracies of the *New York Times* review; your
reviewer is plainly an American neoconservative who
enjoys crude reversals of categories. The American hard
Right has no known interest in the people at large, and a
reverence for the 1 percent that pays for their journals and
think tanks. He refers to my "universally contemptuous
Leftism," which involves "sneering in its disregard for 'the
lower orders . . . the rather shadowy American people.' "
This is the oldest trick in bad book-reviewing. A novelist
writes: " 'I hate America,' shrieked the Communist spy."
This will become, for the dishonest book-reviewer, "At one
point, the author even confesses that he hates America."
But I know of no "Leftist" (define) who sneers at the
people, while no populist could. Rather I concentrate on
what has been done to the people by the 1 percent
through its mastery of the national wealth and made-in-
the-house, as it were, Opinion. Your reviewer even misun-
derstands my own sharp conclusion that an era ended,
happily in my view, when the traditional American ser-
vant class ceased to exist, thanks to the 13 million of us in
the armed services and the full employment of women in

the Second World War. That some of my sillier grandees
mourn this state of affairs is a part of the social comedy of
the narrative, admittedly not of quite so high an order as
the inadvertent comedy of Rightists affecting unrequited
passion for Demos.

The final myth is that Stalin started the Cold War by
dividing Germany into two sections, while trying to drive
us out of our sector of Berlin. I'll quote the best authority,
thus far, on what Truman was up to after Potsdam when he
met Stalin, who, after Yalta, had expected to live in some
sort of reasonable balance with the U.S. Here is Carolyn
Eisenberg in *Drawing the Line: The American Decision to
Divide Germany, 1944–1949* (1996):

> With the inception of the Berlin blockade, Pres-
> ident Truman articulated a simple story that fea-
> tured the Russians trampling the wartime
> agreements in their ruthless grab for the former
> German capital. The President did not explain
> that the United States had [unilaterally—my
> adverb] abandoned Yalta and Potsdam, that it
> was pushing the formation of a Western German
> state against the misgivings of many Europeans
> and that the Soviets had launched the blockade
> to prevent partition.

This great lie remains with us today. Please, no letters about the horrors of the Gulag, Stalin's mistreatment of the buffer states, and so on. Our subject is the serious distortions of the truth on our side and why, unless they are straightened out, we are forever doomed to thrash about in a permanent uncomprehending fog. Good morning, Vietnam!

The attitude towards truth on the part of Truman's administration was best expressed by his Secretary of State, Dean Acheson, in the memoir *Present at the Creation: My Years in the State Department* (1969). It was Acheson who launched the global empire on February 27, 1947. Place: Cabinet Room of the White House. Present: Truman, Secretary of State Marshall, Under Secretary Acheson, a half-dozen Congressional leaders. The British had, yet again, run out of money. They could not honor their agreements to keep Greece tethered to freedom. Could we take over? Although Stalin had warned the Greek Communists that their country was in the U.S. sphere and they should therefore expect no aid from him, Truman wanted a military buildup. We had to stand tall. But Marshall failed to convince the Congressional leaders. Acheson, a superb corporate lawyer and a most witty man, leaped into the breach. He was impassioned. The free world stood at the brink. Yes, at Armageddon. Should the Russians occupy Greece and then Turkey, three continents would be at risk. He used the evergreen homely metaphor of how one rotten apple in a barrel could . . . Finally, were we not the heirs of the Roman Empire? Was not the Soviet Union our Carthage? Had not our Punic Wars begun? We dared not lose. "America has no choice. We must act now to protect our security . . . to protect freedom itself." It was then agreed that if Truman addressed the country in these terms and scared the hell out of the American people, Congress would finance what has turned out to be a half-century of Cold War, costing, thus far, some $7.1 trillion.

In retrospect, Acheson wrote, cheerfully, "If we did make our points clearer than truth, we did not differ from most other educators and could hardly do otherwise." After all, as he noted, it was the State Department's view that the average American spent no more than ten minutes a day brooding on foreign policy; he spends less now that television advertising can make anything clearer than truth.

Today, we are not so much at the brink as fallen over it. Happily, as of this election, we were not at our old stamping ground, Armageddon. Rather, we were simply fretting about fibs involving drunken driving and the true cost of that mother-in-law's medicine as opposed to the pampered dog's, when, had the candidate been true to his roots, he could have found, in a back alley of Carthage, Tennessee, two pinches of cheap sulphur that would have dewormed both mother-in-law and dog in a jiffy.*

The Times Literary Supplement
November 10, 2000

It should be remembered that J. Q. Adams complained of Thomas Jefferson's "large stories." Example? Jefferson claimed to have learned Spanish in nineteen days aboard a transatlantic ship.

JAPANESE INTENTIONS IN THE
SECOND WORLD WAR

S ir,—I am in Clive James's debt for the succinct way
that he has assembled what must be at least 90 percent of all the Received Opinion having to do with
the start and finish of the American-Japanese war of
1941–45 (Letters, November 24). Were it not for occasional
Jacobean resonances, one might suspect that Dr. Barry
Humphries had been working overtime in his bat-hung lab,
assembling yet another Australian monster: a retired Lt.
Col. with a powerful worldview fueled by the tabloid press
of Oz.

James begins briskly: Vidal has an "admonitory vision"
to the effect that the "leadership class" of the American
empire thinks "that Washington is the center of the world.
Unfortunately, Vidal seems to think the same."

Indeed they do. Indeed I do. Indeed, Washington has
been the uncontested global center for most of the twentieth

century, which I tend to deplore—Washington's primacy, that is. In a recent book, *The Golden Age*, I concentrate on the decade 1940–50 when the New World gave birth to the global arrangement.

I start with the convergence on Washington of more than three thousand British agents, propagandists, spies. Yes, I was there. At the heart of an isolationist family that "entertained," as they used to say, every one, I personally observed the brilliant John Foster in action. Foster was attached to Lord Lothian's British embassy. He enchanted the Washingtonians while secretly working with Ben Cohen, a White House lawyer, to draft the Lend-Lease agreement which proved to be the first blow that President Roosevelt was able to strike for England. Residents of that other center, Canberra, no doubt have a different tale to tell.

I make the hardly original case that Franklin Roosevelt provoked the Japanese into attacking us for reasons that I shall come to presently.

James, armed to the teeth with Received Opinion (henceforth RO), tells us that Japan was provoked into war by the Japanese army, "which had been in a position to blackmail the Cabinet since 1922 and never ceased to do so until surrender in 1945," brought on, as RO has it, by gallant Harry Truman's decision to drop a pair of atomic bombs. None of this conforms to what we have known for some time about the internal workings of Japan's intricate system of governance, not to mention our own. There was indeed a gung-ho Japanese military war party that was busy trying to conquer as much of China as possible en route to Southeast Asia where the oil was. There was also a peace party, headed by Prince Konoye, who was eager, as of August 1941, to meet with FDR, who kept postponing a face-to-face discussion to sort out differences. Had FDR been interested in peace in the Pacific, he could have met with Konoye, much as he was secretly meeting with Churchill on a soon-to-be-related matter.

James correctly notes that we had broken Japan's diplomatic code, Purple, but he seems unaware that, by early October 1940, we had also broken many of the Japanese military codes, specifically parts of the Kaigun Ango: the twenty-nine separate naval codes which gave us a good idea of what their fleet was up to during the entire year before Pearl Harbor. RO assures James that, if FDR wanted war, he would not have sent the Emperor, on December 6, a cable whose only message seemed to be a wistful hope that the Japanese would not try to replace the defeated French in Indo-China. James seems ignorant of the context of that message.

Here it is. On Saturday, November 15, 1941, General

Marshall, the U.S. Army Chief of Staff, called in various Washington newspaper bureau chiefs. After swearing them to secrecy, he told them that we had broken Japan's naval codes, and that war with Japan would start sometime during the first ten days of December. On November 26, Cordell Hull, FDR's Secretary of State, presented Japan's two special envoys to Washington with a ten-point proposal, intended, as Hull told Secretary of War Stimson, "to kick the whole thing over." Of FDR's ultimatum, Hull later remarked, "We [had] no serious thought Japan would accept. . . ." What was the proposal? Complete Japanese withdrawal from China and Indo-China, Japan to support China's Nationalist Government and to abandon the tripartite agreement with the Axis. FDR had dropped a shoe. Now he waited for the Japanese to drop the other. They did. RO has it that we were taken by surprise. Certainly, FDR was not. But apparently the unwarned military commanders at Pearl Harbor were, and three thousand men were killed in a single strike.

RO always had a difficult time with motive. Since FDR could never, ever, have set us up, why would the Japanese want to attack a wealthy continental nation four thousand miles away? Fortunately, RO can always fall back on the demonic view of history. As a race, the Japanese were prone to suicide. Hardly human, they were a bestial people whose eyes were so configured that they could never handle modern aircraft or bombsights. As a young soldier in the Pacific, I was, along with everyone else, marinated in this racist nonsense. But should this demonic reading of the Japanese character not be true, one must wonder why the Japanese military, with a difficult war of conquest in China that was using up their wealth and energy in every sense, would want to provoke a war with the United States so far away? RO has had sixty years to come up with an answer; and failed to do so.

Today, no one seriously contests that FDR wanted the U.S. in the war against Hitler. But 60 to 80 percent of the American people were solidly against any European war. In November 1940, FDR had been elected to a third term with the pledge that none of America's sons would ever fight in a foreign war "unless attacked." Privately, more than once, he had said to others that the Japs must strike the first blow or, as he put it to Admiral James O. Richardson (October 8, 1940), "as the war continued and the area of operations expanded, sooner or later they would make a mistake and we would enter the war"; hence, FDR's series of provocations culminating not in a Japanese "mistake" but in the ultimatum of November 26 that left the Japanese with no alternative but war, preferably with a "sneak" knockout attack of the sort that had succeeded so well against Russia in 1904, at Port Arthur. Did FDR know that the Japanese would attack Pearl Harbor, where much of our Pacific fleet was at anchor? Or did he think they would strike at some lesser venue like Manila? This matter is, yet again, under scrutiny.

James's RO is correct when he notes that the German-Italian-Japanese tripartite agreement was of a defensive nature. They were not obliged to join in each other's offensive wars. Why Hitler declared war upon the U.S. is still a "puzzle," according to no less a historian than Dr. Henry Kissinger, not a bad historian when not obliged to gaze into a mirror (cf. his *Diplomacy*).

At war at least in the Pacific, how could FDR be so sure that he would get his war in Europe? Well, FDR is easily the most intricate statesman of our time: as Nixon once said admiringly of Eisenhower, "He was a far more sly and devious man than most people suspected, and I mean those words in their very best sense."

Once the U.S. was wholeheartedly at war on December 8, 1941, our artful dodger could, under wartime powers, aid Britain and the Soviets, as he was already doing with Lend-Lease and other virtuous if quasi-legal measures. Also, FDR's problem with his election pledge ceased to exist when the Japanese responded so fiercely to his provocations and ultimatums. As usual, he got what he wanted.

Received Opinion: without Truman's pair of atom bombs, the famous Japanese war party that had seized control of the government would have ordered a million Japanese to jump off cliffs onto the invading Americans had not the Emperor, distressed by the bombs, etc. . . . Let us turn from comfortable RO to Authority, to Ambassador Joseph C. Grew's memoir, *Turbulent Era: A Diplomatic Record of Forty Years, 1904–1945*. As U.S. Ambassador to Japan, Grew was dedicated to bringing together FDR and Prince Konoye, little suspecting that, where Konoye was apparently sincere in wanting peace, FDR was not. By autumn 1941, Grew was exasperated by Washington's unrelenting line that the Japanese government was completely dominated by the military war party:

> We in Tokyo were closer to the scene than was the Administration in Washington and we believed, on the basis of the highest possible intelligence, and so reported, that the Japanese government at the time was in a position to control the armed forces of the country. We explained in several of our telegrams to our Government that Germany's attack on Soviet Russia had given those elements in Japan which controlled national policies further and convincing

> evidence that confidence could not be placed in
> Germany's promises. . . . No one, I think, would
> contest the view that the Japanese government
> was in a far better position to control its forces
> in the summer of 1941 than it was in December
> 1938. . . .

The problem with RO, even when served up by so sensitive a writer as Clive James, is that contrary evidence must not be admitted. RO still clings to the myth that Japan would have fought to the end if Truman had not dropped his A-bombs. But Japanese envoys had been making overtures for a year in, variously, Sweden, Switzerland, Portugal, the Vatican, etc. Message: the war is over if the Emperor is retained.

Finally, the most important Japanese player, as I noted in my piece (November 10), the Emperor himself, on July 18, 1945, wrote Truman a letter "looking for peace" (Truman's words). On August 3, 1945, an official's diary notes that Truman, Byrnes, and Leahy were discussing a telegram "from the Emperor asking for peace." Truman, inspired, some believe, by Secretary of State Byrnes, wanted to intimidate the Soviets with our super-weapon. So he had his two big bangs, contrary to the advice of his chief military commanders. Here is Eisenhower: "I had been conscious of a feeling of depression and so I voiced to [Secretary of War Henry L. Stimson] my grave misgivings. . . . I thought that our country should avoid shocking world opinion by the use of a weapon whose employment was, I thought, no longer mandatory as a measure to save American lives."

FDR, like so many Americans of his generation, found irresistible the phrase "unconditional surrender"—General U. S. Grant's adamantine message to the Confederacy. FDR applied it to the Axis powers. Truman inherited this policy. Then, once he had dropped his bombs, he promptly abandoned unconditional surrender and kept the Emperor. For Clive of Canberra, I recommend the latest, if not last, word on the subject, *The Decision to Use the Atomic Bomb and the Architecture of an American Myth* by Gar Alperovitz. For the why and what of Pearl Harbor, there is now R. B. Stinnett's *Day of Deceit*, soon to be a subject of strenuous debate in another journal.

Again, how could FDR have known Hitler would declare war on us after Pearl Harbor? James's RO provides him with no sensible motive. So he falls back on the demonic— "megalomania," which drove Hitler to ensure that he would be at war on every side. But this won't do. Hitler was certainly subject to fits of inspiration, but he was usually very cautious in his dealings with the "mongrel" Americans. In his December 11 declaration of war to the Reichstag, he gave a seemingly rational if odd reason. On December 4, at the President's request, General Marshall had presented FDR with a war plan in which he proposed that, as Hitler was the principal enemy of the U.S. and the world, the United States should raise an expeditionary force of 5 million men and send it to invade Germany by July 1, 1943. The plan—one hopes of no more than a contingency nature—was leaked onto the front page of the *Chicago Tribune*, the great trumpet of isolationism. The headline, "F.D.R.'S WAR PLANS!" Three days later, Pearl Harbor erased the story, but Hitler had seen it and mentioned it as "proof" of FDR's predatory designs on the Axis, noting (more in sorrow than in anger?), "Without any attempt at an official denial on the part of the American Government, President Roosevelt's plan has been published under which Germany and Italy are to be attacked with military force in Europe by 1943 at the latest." (This is from *A World to Gain* by Thomas Toughill, an intriguing amateur sleuth.)

Finally, for an analysis of the persisting myth about the dropping of the A-bombs, Mr. Alperovitz is hearteningly shrewd.

The Times Literary Supplement
December 1, 2000

*   *   *

Sir,—When Kenneth Tynan came to New York to practice his trade as drama critic, he had only recently become a Marxist. Brecht had had something to do with it, and I think he may have read some of Marx. Certainly he often quoted him, usually at midpoint during one of our late evenings at the Mayfair workers' canteen, Mirabelle. "Money should not breed money," Ken would stammer. Upon arrival in New York, he began to evangelize. I watched him with an ancient *Partisan Review* editor, a former Stalinist, Trotskyite, Reichian. Fiercely, Ken told him what it was that money must never do. When Ken had run out of breath, the weary old class warrior said, "Mr. Tynan, your arguments are so old that I have forgotten all the answers to them."

The estimable Clive James (Letters, December 8) is in a time warp similar to Ken's. Thirty years of incremental information about the American-Japanese war have passed him by. He thinks "the real [Japanese] fleet sent no radio messages" en route to Pearl Harbor: that "was long ago invalidated." No. What has been invalidated is the myth that the Japanese kept complete radio silence. In 1993 and 1995 (under the Freedom of Information Act), all sorts of transcripts came to light, as well as Communication Intelligence Summaries such as this one for December 6, 1941, where an American code-breaker reported: "The Commander in Chief

Combined (Japanese) Fleet originated several messages to Carriers, Fourth Fleet and the Major Commanders." Each headed toward Hawaii and interacting. Although there is some evidence that James has kept up with the latest Hirohito books (Chrysanthemum Porn, as we call it in the trade), he has no interest in political revelations. I do. But then I spent five years researching *The Golden Age*, trying to figure out what actually happened at Pearl Harbor, and why the A-bombs were dropped *after* Japan was ready to surrender, and why . . . I shall not repeat myself, but I must note, in passing, the purity of a certain mid-twentieth-century journalistic style that continues to reverberate like the beat beat beat of the tom-tom in Clive of Canberra's burnished prose. Ingredients? High Moral Indignation, no matter how hoked up, linked to *ad hominem* zingers from right field. I referred to the leader of the peace party at the Japanese court, Prince Konoye. I was interested in his proposals. Our period journalist is interested in Konoye as an anti-Semite who faked his own suicide note. Is it possible that I have misjudged Konoye's dedication to peace? Was he also, like so many Japanese princes, an adulterer? If so, was that the reason FDR refused to meet him at Juneau, an Alaskan beauty spot that is, in summer, a breeding ground for the largest mosquitoes in North America? FDR's sense of fun seldom abandoned him. In any case, for whatever reason, after suggesting a comical venue, FDR backed down. Peace in the Pacific was not his dream.

Next, Charles Lindbergh, my "other questionable hero," is dragged in, so that we can be told, with righteous anger, how "his isolationism was *de facto* an instrument of Axis policy." Surely James the Latinist means *ad hoc* in a sentence admittedly quite as meaningless as that tom-tom pounding you you you. He does admit that "Lindbergh did loyal service [in the war] and even shot down a Japanese plane but [one] can't help wondering about the American planes he shot down with his mouth"; moral outrage is now in high gear—pass me the sick bag, Alice, or whatever that splendid gel was called. In real life, Lindbergh was sent by FDR to take a look at the German air force and plane production. Lindbergh was sufficiently alarmed by what he saw to urge increased American production of aircraft for war, particularly the B-17. He was, of course, an isolationist, and so was reflective of a majority of the American people before Pearl Harbor.

Then, alas, we hear that "Ambassador Joseph Grew, alas, won't do for a hero either." Plainly my world contained no heroes. Although Grew was much admired for his brilliance and probity by those of us who had relations with him, the great Canberra moralist tells us that he was worse than an anti-Semite, he was a snob. Could it be that this terrible flaw in his character encouraged the war party in Tokyo to attack the United States? But Mr. James—again, alas—never connects his enticing dots. Actually, Grew's problem as a diplomat was that he tried to maintain the peace between Japan and the U.S., when his President had other plans which involved maneuvering the Japanese into striking the first blow so that we could go to war. But then James always dodges the great unanswered question: unless provoked by us, *why did the Japanese attack?* He waffles a bit about their desire for "unopposed expansion." To where? Chicago?

Finally, a rhetorical question to me. If I had been told in 1945 that we had a weapon "so devastating that it could end that . . . war in a week," what would I have said? Well, none of us was consulted. But we were, most of us, highly in favor of using the Bomb. On the other hand, had we been told that the war could have been concluded as of May 1945, I would have gone to work for the impeachment of a President who had wasted so many lives and destroyed so many cities in his power game with the Soviet Union which led, inexorably, to a half-century of unnecessary Cold War. I am also bemused that a witness so all-knowing, if not knowledgeable, as Clive James, still doesn't understand what happened to him, to all of us, for most of our lives.

The Times Literary Supplement
December 15, 2000

How We Missed the
Saturday Dance

Duke Ellington on the jukebox: "Missed the Saturday dance, heard they crowded the floor, duh duh duh-duh . . ." I can almost carry a tune but I can't remember the words to any song, including the inspired lyrics of our national anthem. But this song, and those notes, have been sounding in my head for over half a century, ever since I heard them at a dance hall near the army camp where I was stationed.

Just out of Exeter, I had enlisted in the army at seventeen. That was a year after George Bush, just out of Andover, enlisted in the navy. Most important, my best friend from a Washington, D.C., school enlisted in the Marine Corps. He had been "safe" at Duke: he had a contract to be a professional baseball player when the war was over. But he thought that he should go fight too. He became a scout and observer for the Third Marine Division in the Pacific. He saw action at Guam. He was assigned to "Operation Detachment" and shipped out to Iwo Jima, where the Japanese were entrenched in tunnels beneath that bleak island's surface.

On February 19, 1945, the Marines landed on Iwo Jima, after a long, fairly futile aerial bombardment. The Japanese were out of reach belowground. On D-Day plus nine, elements of the Third Division landed on the already crowded island, eight square miles of volcanic ash and rock. Like the skull of some prehistoric brontosaurus Mount Suribachi looms over the five-and-a-half-mile-long island. Lately, I have been watching closely each frame of an old newsreel that now seems so long ago that it might as well be a series of Brady stills from Antietam, except for the fact that it is still as immediate to me as yesterday, even though I was not there but on another Pacific island, far to the north in the Bering Sea. It took a month to win the island. Twenty thousand Japanese were killed; 6,821 American troops, mostly marines, were killed. On D-Day plus ten, March 1, 1945, at 4:15 A.M., Pvt. James Trimble was killed instantly by a grenade. He was nineteen years old. Bush and I survived.

It is somehow fitting that our generation—the war generation, as we think, perhaps too proudly, of ourselves—should be officially as well as actuarially at an end with the replacement of George Bush by a man who could be his—

our—son. I say fitting because our generation, which won in battle the American Empire, is somehow nicely epitomized by the career of Bush, who served with energetic mindlessness the empire, always managing, whenever confronted with a fork in the road of our imperial destiny, to take, as did his predecessors, the wrong turning.

Elsewhere, I have noted that the American Golden Age lasted only five years: from war's end, 1945, to 1950, the Korean War's start. During this interval the arts flourished and those of us who had missed our youth tried to catch up. Meanwhile, back at the White House, unknown to us, the managers of the new world empire were hard at work replacing the republic for which we had fought with a secret National Security State, pledged to an eternal war with communism in general and the Soviet Union in particular. It is true that Harry Truman and our other managers feared that if we did not remain on a wartime footing we might drift back into the Great Depression that had not ended until the Japanese attacked us at Pearl Harbor, and everyone went to war or work. It is part of the national myth that the attack was unprovoked. Actually, we had been spoiling for a war with Japan since the beginning of the century. Was the Pacific—indeed Asia—to be theirs or ours? Initially, the Japanese preferred to conquer mainland Asia. But when it looked as if we might deny them access to

Southeast Asian oil, they attacked. Had they not, we would never have gone to war, in the Pacific or in Europe.

I was born eight years after the end of the First World War. As I was growing up, it was well remembered that we had got nothing out of that war in Europe except an attack on the Bill of Rights at home and, of course, the noble experiment, Prohibition. Young people often ask me, with wonder, why so many of us enlisted in 1943. I tell them that since we had been attacked at Pearl Harbor, we were obliged to defend our country. But I should note that where, in 1917, millions of boys were eager to go fight the Hun, we were not eager. We were fatalistic. In the three years that I spent in the army, I heard no soldier express a patriotic sentiment; rather the reverse, when we saw the likes of Errol Flynn on the screen winning freedom's war, or, even worse, John Wayne, known to us by his real name, Marion, the archetypal draft-dodging actor who, to rub it in, impersonated a Flying Tiger in the movies.

Although we were not enthusiastic warriors, there was a true hatred of the enemy. We were convinced that the "Japs" were subhuman; and our atrocities against them pretty much matched theirs against us. I was in the Pacific Theater of Operations, where the war was not only imperial but racial: the white race was fighting the yellow race, and the crown would go to us as we were the earth's supreme race, or so we had been taught. One of the ugliest aspects of that war was the racial stereotyping on both sides. In Europe we were respectful—even fearful—of the Germans. Since blacks and women were pretty much segregated in our military forces, World War II was, for us, literally, the white man's burden.

So while the Golden Age had its moment in the sun up on deck, down in the engine room the management was inventing the "Defense" Department and the National Security Council with its secret, unconstitutional decrees, and the equally unconstitutional CIA, modeled, Allen Dulles remarked blithely, on the Soviets' NKVD. We were then, without public debate, committed to a never-ending war, even though the management knew that the enemy was no match for us, economically or militarily. But, through relentless CIA "disinformation," they managed to convince us that what was weak was strong, and that the Russians were definitely coming. "Build backyard shelters against the coming atomic war!" A generation was well and truly traumatized.

The Korean War put an end to our title as invincible heavyweight military champion of the world. We might have maintained our mystique by avoiding this eccentric war (we did call it a "police action"), but by then we had so exaggerated the power of the Soviet Union in tandem with

China that we could do nothing but reel from one point-less military confrontation to another.

Unfortunately, Kennedy was less cynically practical than those who had presided over what Dean Acheson called "the creation" of the empire. Kennedy actually believed—or pretended to believe—their rhetoric. He liked the phrase "this twilight time." He believed in the domino theory. He believed in "bearing any burden." He invaded Cuba, and failed. He turned his attention to Asia, to "contain China" by interfering in a Vietnamese civil war where a majority had already voted for the communist Ho Chi Minh, who, quoting Jefferson, asked Eisenhower to make Vietnam an American protectorate. But, as Ike explained in his mem-oirs, this wasn't possible: they were Communists.

In June 1961 Kennedy began the fastest buildup mili-tarily since Pearl Harbor; he also rearmed Germany, setting off alarm bells in the Soviet Union. They spoke of denying us land access to our section of Berlin. Kennedy responded with a warlike speech, invoking "the Berlin crisis" as a world crisis. In response, Khrushchev built the wall. It was as if we were, somehow, willing a war to turn sad twilight to incandescent nuclear high noon.

The missile crisis in Cuba was the next move, with us as the provocateurs. Then, with the Vietnam War, we not only took the wrong road, we went straight around the bend, fighting the longest war in our history in a region where we had no strategic interest unless we were to openly declare what the management, then and now, does truly believe: the United States is the master of the earth and anyone who defies us will be napalmed or blockaded or covertly over-thrown. We are beyond law, which is not unusual for an empire; unfortunately, we are also beyond common sense.

The only subject, other than the deficit, that should have been discussed in the late election was the military budget. Neither Bush nor Clinton came anywhere close. Eventually, we shall be unable to borrow enough money to preen ourselves in ever weaker countries, but until then, thanks to the many suicidal moves made by that imperial generation forged in the Second World War, our country is now not so much divided as in pieces.

The latest managerial wit has been to encourage—by deploring—something called "political correctness," this decade's Silly Putty or Hula Hoop. Could anything be better calculated to divert everyone from what the management is up to in recently appropriating, say, $3.8 billion for SDI than to pit sex against sex, race against race, religion against religion? With everyone in arms against everyone else, no one will have the time to take arms against the ruinously expensive empire that Mr. Clinton and the unattractively named baby boomers have inherited. I wish them luck.

There are those who sentimentalize the Second World War. I don't. There can be no "good war." We set out to stop Germany and Japan from becoming hemispheric powers. Now, of course, they are economic world powers while we, with our $4 trillion of debt, look to be joining Argentina and Brazil on the outer edge. All in all, the famed good, great war that gave us the empire that we then proceeded to make a mess of was hardly worth the death of one Pvt. James Trimble USMCR, much less the death of millions of others.

I have just listened to the original Duke Ellington record. Here are those lyrics that I always forget:

"Missed the Saturday dance, heard they crowded the floor, couldn't bear it without you, don't get around much anymore." All in all, it's a good thing for the world that with Bush's departure we don't get around much anymore. Somalia-Bosnia could be the last of our hurrahs, produced by CNN and, so far, sponsorless. Maybe now, without us, Clinton's generation will make it to the Saturday dance that we missed. And let's hope that the floor won't prove to be too crowded with rivals in trade if not in love, death.

Newsweek
January 11, 1993

THE LAST EMPIRE

I t is wonderful indeed, ladies and gentlemen, to have all of you here between covers, as it were—here being the place old John Bunyan called "Vanity Fair, because the town where 'tis kept, is lighter than vanity."* But these days the town is not so much London or New York as the global village itself, wherein you are this month's movers and shakers, as well as moved and shaken (I feel your pain, Yasser). In a number of ways I find it highly fitting that we meet on the old fairground as twentieth century and Second Christian Millennium are saying goodbye. Personally, I thought they'd never go without taking us with them. There are, of course, 791 days still to go. I also note that the photographers have immortalized a number of smiles. Joy? Or are those anthropologists right who say that the human baring of teeth signals aggression? Let's hope not before 2001 C.E.

*The *Vanity Fair* issue of December 1999 featured photographs of all the leaders as well as this text.

Of course, centuries and millennia are just arbitrary markings, like bookkeeping at Paramount Pictures. But, symbolically, they mean a lot to those who are interested in why we are today what we are and doing what we are doing. This goes particularly for those movers and shakers who have spent a lot of this year in meetings, courtesy of the one indisposable—or did President Clinton say indispensable?—nation on earth and last self-styled global power, loaded down with nukes, bases, debts.

Denver and Madrid were two fairgrounds. Nothing much is ever accomplished when the managing world director calls in his regional directors for fun and frolic. But when Clinton chose a cowboy theme at Denver, with boots for all, some regional directors actually dared whine. But they are easily replaced and know it. Later the Seven Leading Economic Powers (plus Russia) decided, at Madrid, to extend the North Atlantic Treaty Organization to include Poland, Czechland, Hungary. Jacques Chirac, the French director of the . . . well, let's be candid: American Empire . . . wanted several more Eastern countries to join, while the Russian director wanted *no* Eastern extension of a military alliance that he still thinks, mistakenly, was formed to protect Eastern Europe from the power-mad Soviet Union. Actually, as we shall see, NATO was created so that the United States could dominate *Western* Europe militarily, politically, and economically; any current extension means that more nations and territories will come under American control while giving pleasure to such hyphenate American voters as Poles, Czechs, Hungarians. The French director was heard to use the word *merde* when the American emperor said that only three new countries are to be allowed in this time. The Frenchman was ignored, but then he had lost an election back home. In any case, the North Atlantic confederation of United States–Canada plus Western Europe can now be called the North Atlantic Baltic Danubian Organization, to which the Caspian Sea will no doubt soon be added.

I see that some of you are stirring impatiently. The United States is *an empire*? The emperor's advisers chuckle at the notion. Are we not a freedom-loving perfect democracy eager to exhibit our state-of-the-art economy to old Europe as a model of what you can do in the way of making money for the few by eliminating labor unions and such decadent frills as public health and education? At Denver a French spear-carrier—always those pesky French—wondered just how reliable our unemployment figures were when one-tenth of the male workforce is not counted, as they are either in prison or on probation or parole. The Canadian prime minister, even more tiresome than the French, was heard to say to his Belgian counterpart (over an open mike) that if the leaders of any other country took corporate money as openly as American leaders do, "we'd be in jail." Plainly, the natives are restive. But we are still in charge of the Vanity Fair.

I bring up all this not to be unkind. Rather, I should like to point out that those who live too long with unquestioned contradictions are not apt to be able to deal with reality when it eventually befalls them. I have lived through nearly three-quarters of this century. I enlisted in the army of the United States at seventeen; went to the Pacific; did nothing useful—I was just there, as Nixon used to say, WHEN THE BOMBS WERE FALLING. But, actually, the bombs were not really falling on either of us: he was a naval officer making a fortune playing poker, while I was an army first mate writing a novel.

Now, suddenly, it's 1997, and we are "celebrating" the fiftieth anniversary of the Truman Doctrine and the Marshall Plan. Also, more ominously, July 26 was the fiftieth anniversary of the National Security Act that, without national debate but very quiet bipartisan Congressional support, replaced the old American Republic with a National Security State very much in the global-empire business, which explains . . .

But, first, into the Time Machine.

It is the Ides of August 1945. Germany and Japan have

surrendered, and some 13 million Americans are headed home to enjoy—well, being alive was always the bottom line. Home turns out to be a sort of fairground where fireworks go off and the band plays "Don't Sit Under the Apple Tree," and an endlessly enticing fun house flings open its doors and we file through. We enjoy halls of mirrors where everyone is comically distorted, ride through all the various tunnels of love, and take scary tours of horror chambers where skeletons and cobwebs and bats brush past us until, suitably chilled and thrilled, we are ready for the exit and everyday life, but, to the consternation of some—and the apparent indifference of the rest—we were never allowed to leave the fun house entirely: it had become a part of our world, as were the goblins sitting under that apple tree.

Officially, the United States was at peace; much of Europe and most of Japan were in ruins, often literally, certainly economically. We alone had all our cities and a sort of booming economy—"sort of" because it depended on war production, and there was, as far as anyone could tell, no war in the offing. But the arts briefly flourished. *The Glass Menagerie* was staged, Copland's *Appalachian Spring* was played. A film called *The Lost Weekend*—not a bad title for what we had gone through—won an Academy Award, and the as yet un-exiled Richard Wright published a much-admired novel, *Black Boy*, while Edmund Wilson's novel

Memoirs of Hecate County was banned for obscenity in parts of the country. Quaintly, each city had at least three or four daily newspapers in those days, while New York, as befitted *the* world city, had seventeen newspapers. But a novelty, television, had begun to appear in household after household, its cold gray distorting eye relentlessly projecting a fun-house view of the world.

Those who followed the—ugly new-minted word— media began to note that while watching even Milton Berle we kept fading in and out of the Chamber of Horrors. Subliminal skeletons would suddenly flash onto the TV screen; our ally in the recent war, "Uncle Joe Stalin," as the accidental President Harry S Truman had called him, was growing horns and fangs that dripped blood. On earth, we were the only great unruined power with atomic weapons; yet we were now—somehow—at terrible risk. Why? How?

The trouble appeared to be over Germany, which, on February 11, 1945, had been split at the Yalta summit meeting into four zones: American, Soviet, British, French. As the Russians had done the most fighting and suffered the greatest losses, it was agreed that they should have an early crack at reparations from Germany—to the extent of $20 billion. At a later Potsdam meeting the new President Truman, with Stalin and Churchill, reconfirmed Yalta and opted for the unification of Germany under the four victorious powers. But something had happened between the euphoria of Yalta and the edginess of Potsdam. As the meeting progressed, the atom bomb was tried out successfully in a New Mexico desert. We were now able to incinerate Japan—or the Soviet, for that matter—and so we no longer needed Russian help to defeat Japan. We started to renege on our agreements with Stalin, particularly reparations from Germany. We also quietly shelved the notion, agreed upon at Yalta, of a united Germany under four-power control. Our aim now was to unite the three Western zones of Germany and integrate them into *our* Western Europe, restoring, in the process, the German economy—hence, fewer reparations. Then, as of May 1946, we began to rearm Germany. Stalin went ape at this betrayal. The Cold War was on.

At home, the media were beginning to prepare the attentive few for Disappointment. Suddenly, we were faced with the highest personal income taxes in American history to pay for more and more weapons, among them the world-killer hydrogen bomb—all because *the Russians were coming*. No one knew quite why they were coming or with what. Weren't they still burying 20 million dead? Official explanations for all this made little sense, but then, as Truman's secretary of state, Dean Acheson, merrily observed, "In the

State Department we used to discuss how much time that mythical 'average American citizen' put in each day listening, reading, and arguing about the world outside his own country. . . . It seemed to us that ten minutes a day would be a high average." So why bore the people? Secret "bipartisan" government is best for what, after all, is—or should be—a society of docile workers, enthusiastic consumers, obedient soldiers who will believe just about anything for at least ten minutes. The National Security State, the NATO alliance, the forty-year Cold War were all created without the consent, much less advice, of the American people. Of course, there were elections during this crucial time, but Truman-Dewey, Eisenhower-Stevenson, Kennedy-Nixon were of a single mind as to the desirability of inventing, first, a many-tentacled enemy, Communism, the star of the Chamber of Horrors; then, to combat so much evil, installing a permanent wartime state at home with loyalty oaths, a national "peacetime" draft, and secret police to keep watch over homegrown "traitors," as the few enemies of the National Security State were known. Then followed forty years of mindless wars which created a debt of $5 trillion that hugely benefited aerospace and firms like General Electric, whose longtime TV pitchman was Ronald Reagan, eventually retired to the White House.

Why go into all this now? Have we not done marvelously

well as the United States of Amnesia? Our economy is the envy of the earth, the President proclaimed at Denver. No inflation. Jobs for all except the 3 percent of the population in prison and the 5 percent who no longer look for work and so are not counted, bringing our actual unemployment close to the glum European average of 11 percent. And all of this accomplished without ever once succumbing to the sick socialism of Europe. We have no health service or proper public education or, indeed, much of anything for the residents of the fun house. But there are lots of ill-paid work-hours for husband and wife with no care for the children while parents are away from home. Fortunately, Congress is now preparing legislation so that adult prisons can take in delinquent fourteen-year-olds. They, at least, will be taken care of, while, economically, it is only a matter of time before the great globe itself is green-spanned.

Certainly European bankers envy us our powerless labor unions (only 14 percent of the lucky funsters are privileged to belong to a labor union) and our industries—lean, mean, downsized, with no particular place for the redundant to go except into the hell of sizzle and fry and burn. Today we give orders to other countries. We tell them with whom to trade and to which of our courts they must show up for indictment should they disobey us. Meanwhile, FBI agents range the world looking for drug fiends and peddlers while the unconstitutional CIA (they don't submit their accounts to Congress as the Constitution requires) chases "terrorists" now that their onetime colleagues and sometime paymasters in the Russian KGB have gone out of business.

We have arrived at what Tennessee Williams once called A Moon of Pause. When I asked him what on earth the phrase meant, as spoken by an actress in one of his plays, "It is," he said loftily, "the actual Greek translation of menopause." I said that the word "moon" did not come from *menses* (Latin, not Greek, for "month"). "Then what," he asked suspiciously, "is the Latin for moon?" When I told him it was *luna* and what fun he might have with the word "lunatic," he sighed and cut. But at the time of the Madrid conference about the extension of NATO, a moon of pause seemed a nice dotty phrase for the change of life that our empire is now going through, with no enemy and no discernible function.

While we were at our busiest in the fun house, no one ever told us what the North Atlantic Treaty Alliance was really about. March 17, 1948, the Treaty of Brussels called for a military alliance of Britain, France, Benelux to be joined by the U.S. and Canada on March 23. The impetus behind NATO was the United States, whose principal foreign policy, since the administration of George Washington, was to avoid what Alexander Hamilton called "entangling alliances." Now, as the Russians were supposed to be coming, we replaced the old republic with the newborn National Security State and set up shop as the major *European* power west of the Elbe. We were now hell-bent on the permanent division of Germany between our western zone (plus the French and British zones) and the Soviet zone to the east. Serenely, we broke every agreement that we had made with our former ally, now horrendous Communist enemy. For those interested in the details, Carolyn Eisenberg's *Drawing the Line: The American Decision to Divide Germany 1944-49* is a masterful survey of an empire—sometimes blindly, sometimes brilliantly—assembling itself by turning first its allies and then its enemies like Germany, Italy, Japan into client states, permanently subject to our military and economic diktat.

Although the Soviets still wanted to live by our original agreements at Yalta and even Potsdam, we had decided, unilaterally, to restore the German economy in order to enfold a rearmed Germany into Western Europe, thus isolating the Soviet, a nation which had not recovered from the Second World War and had no nuclear weapons. It was Acheson—again—who elegantly explained all the lies that he was obliged to tell Congress and the ten-minute-attention-spanned average American: "If we did make our points clearer than truth, we did not differ from most other educators and could hardly do otherwise. . . . Qualification must give way to simplicity of statement, nicety and nuance to bluntness, almost brutality, in carrying home a point." Thus were two generations of Americans treated by their overlords until, in the end, at the word "Communism," there is an orgasmic Pavlovian reflex just as the brain goes dead.

In regard to the "enemy," Ambassador Walter Bedell Smith—a former general with powerful simple views—wrote to his old boss General Eisenhower from Moscow in December 1947 apropos a conference to regularize European matters: "The difficulty under which we labor is that in spite of our announced position we really do not want nor intend to accept German unification in any terms the Russians might agree to, even though they seemed to meet most of our requirements." Hence, Stalin's frustration that led to the famous blockade of the Allied section of Berlin, overcome by General Lucius Clay's successful airlift. As Eisenberg writes, "With the inception of the Berlin blockade, President Truman articulated a simple story that featured the Russians, trampling the wartime agreements in their ruthless grab for the former German capital. The President did not explain that the United States had abandoned Yalta and Potsdam, that it was pushing the formation of a West German state against the misgivings of many Europeans, and that the Soviets had launched the blockade to prevent partition." This was fun-house politics at its most tragicomical.

The President, like a distorting mirror, reversed the truth. But then he was never on top of the German situation as opposed to the coming election (November 1948), an election of compelling personal interest to him but, in the great scheme of things, to no one else. He did realize that the few Americans who could identify George Washington might object to our NATO alliance, and so his secretary of state, Acheson, was told to wait until February 1949, *after* the election, to present to Congress our changeover from a Western Hemisphere republic to an imperial European polity, symmetrically balanced by our Asian empire, centered on occupied Japan and, in due course, its tigerish pendant, the ASEAN alliance.

The case for an American world empire was never properly argued, since the debate—what little there was—centered on the alleged desire of the Soviet Union to conquer the whole world, just as Hitler and the Nazis were trying to do until stopped, in 1945, by the Soviet Union with (what Stalin regarded as suspiciously belated) aid from the U.S.

On March 12, 1947, Truman addressed Congress to

proclaim what would be known as the Truman Doctrine, in which he targeted our ally of two years earlier as the enemy. The subject at hand was a civil war in Greece, supposedly directed by the Soviet. We could not tolerate this as, suddenly, "the policy of the United States [is] to support free peoples who are resisting attempted subjugation by armed minorities or by outside pressure." Thus, Truman made the entire world the specific business of the United States. Although the Greek insurgents were getting some help from Bulgaria and Yugoslavia, the Soviet stayed out. They still hoped that the British, whose business Greece had been, would keep order. But as Britain had neither the resources nor the will, she called on the U.S. to step in. Behind the usual closed doors, Acheson was stirring up Congress with Iago-like intensity: Russian pressure of some sort "had brought the Balkans to the point where a highly possible Soviet breakthrough might open three continents to Soviet penetration." Senators gasped; grew pale; wondered how to get more "defense" contracts into their states.

Of the major politicians, only former vice president Henry Wallace dared answer Truman's "clearer than truth" version of history: "Yesterday March 12, 1947, marked a turning point in American history, [for] it is not a Greek crisis that we face, it is an American crisis. Yesterday, President Truman . . . proposed, in effect, that America police

Russia's every border. There is no regime too reactionary for us provided it stands in Russia's expansionist path. There is no country too remote to serve as the scene of a contest which may widen until it becomes a world war."

Nine days after Truman declared war on Communism, he installed a federal loyalty-oath program. All government employees must now swear allegiance to the new order. Wallace struck again: "The President's executive order creates a master index of public servants. From the janitor in the village post office to the Cabinet members, they are to be sifted, and tested and watched and appraised."

Truman was nervously aware that many regarded Wallace as true heir to Roosevelt's New Deal; Wallace was also likely to enter the presidential race of 1948. Truman now left truth behind in the dust. "The attempt of Lenin, Trotsky, Stalin, et al. to fool the world and the American Crackpots Association, represented by Jos. Davies, Henry Wallace, Claude Pepper, and the actors and artists in immoral Greenwich Village, is just like Hitler's and Mussolini's so-called socialist states." Give 'em hell, Harry.

In the wake of Truman's cuckoo-like emergence from the old-fashioned closet of the original American Republic, a new American state was being born in order to save the nation and the great globe itself from Communism. The nature of this militarized state was, from the beginning, beyond rational debate. Characteristically, Truman and Acheson insisted on closed hearings of the Senate Committee on Foreign Relations. These matters were too important to share with the people whose spare ten minutes was now more and more filling up with television. The committee's Republican leader, Arthur H. Vandenberg, the great goose of Grand Rapids, Michigan, was thrilled to be taken into the confidence of the creators of the new empire, but he did suggest that, practically speaking, if hell wasn't scared out of the American people, Congress would have a hard time raising the revenues to pay for a military buildup in what was still thought to be, inside the ever more isolated fun house, peacetime. The media spoke with a single voice. Time Inc. publisher Henry Luce said it loudest: "God had founded America as a global beacon of freedom." Dissenters, like Wallace, were labeled Communists and ceased to engage meaningfully in public life or, by 1950, even in debate. Like the voice of a ghost, an ancestral voice, he spoke on May 21, 1947: "Today in blind fear of communism, we are turning aside from the United Nations. We are approaching a century of fear." Thus far, he is proved to be half right.

On July 26, 1947, Congress enacted the National Security Act, which created the National Security Council, still going strong, and the Central Intelligence Agency, still apparently going over a cliff as the result of decades of bad intelligence, not to mention all those cheery traitors for whom the country club at Langley, Virginia, was once an impenetrable cover. Years later, a sadder, if not wiser, Truman told his biographer, Merle Miller, that the CIA had become a dangerous mess and ought not to have been set up as it was. But in 1947 the CIA's principal role in Europe was not to counter Soviet activities but to control the politics of NATO members. French and Italian trade unions and publications were subsidized, and a great deal of secret money was poured into Italy to ensure the victory of the Christian Democratic Party in the elections of April 1948.

Acheson, in *Present at the Creation*, a memoir that compensates in elegance what it lacks in candor, alludes delicately to National Security Council document 68 (the 1950 blueprint for our war against Communism). But in 1969, when he was writing, he sadly notes that the memo is still classified. Only in 1975 was it to be declassified. There are seven points. First, never negotiate with the Soviet Union. No wonder the rebuffed Stalin, ever touchy, kept reacting brutally in Mitteleuropa. Second, develop the hydrogen bomb so that when the Russians go atomic we will still be ahead of them. Third, rapidly build up conventional forces.

Fourth, to pay for this, levy huge personal income taxes—as high as 90 percent. Fifth, mobilize everyone in the war against internal Communism through propaganda, loyalty oaths, and spy networks like the FBI, whose secret agent Ronald Reagan, President of the Screen Actors Guild, had come into his splendid own, fingering better actors. Sixth, set up a strong alliance system, directed by the United States—NATO. Seventh, make the people of Russia, through propaganda and CIA derring-do, our allies against their government, thus legitimizing, with this highly vague task, our numerous unaccountable secret agents.

So, after five years in the fun house, we partially emerged in January 1950, to find ourselves in a new sort of country. We were also, astonishingly, again at war: this time in Korea. But as Truman-Acheson were nervous about asking Congress for a declaration, the war was called a United Nations police action; and messily lost. Acheson did prepare a memo assuring Truman that, hitherto, eighty-seven presidential military adventures had been undertaken without a Congressional declaration of war as required by the old Constitution. Since 1950 the United States has fought perhaps a hundred overt and covert wars. None was declared by the nominal representatives of the American People in Congress Assembled; they had meekly turned over to the executive their principal great power, to wage war. That was the end of that Constitution.

As it will take at least a decade for us to reinvent China as a new evil empire, the moon is in a state of pause over the old fairground. We are entering a phase undreamed of by those "present at the creation" of the empire. Although many still reflexively object to the word "empire," we have military bases in every continent, as well as ten aboard the aircraft carrier called the United Kingdom. For fifty years we have supported too many tyrants, overthrown too many democratic governments, wasted too much of our own money in other people's civil wars to pretend that we're just helping out all those poor little folks around the world who love freedom and democracy just like we do. When the Russians stabbed us in the back by folding their empire in 1991, we were left with many misconceptions about ourselves and, rather worse, about the rest of the world.

The literature on what we did and why since 1945 is both copious and thin. There are some first-rate biographies of the various players. If one goes digging, there are interesting monographs like Walter LaFeber's "NATO and the Korean War: A Context." But the link between universities and imperial Washington has always been a strong one as Kissingers dart back and forth between classroom to high office to even higher, lucrative eminence, as lobbyists for foreign powers, often hostile to our interests. Now, with Carolyn Eisenberg's *Drawing the Line*, there is a step-by-step description of the years 1944–49, when we restored, rearmed, and reintegrated *our* German province into *our* Western Europe. For those who feel that Eisenberg dwells too much on American confusions and mendacities, there is always the elegant Robert H. Ferrell on "The Formation of the Alliance, 1948–1949." A court historian, as apologists for empire are known, Ferrell does his best with Harry Truman, reminding us of all the maniacs around him who wanted atomic war at the time of Korea, among them the first secretary of defense, the paranoid James Forrestal, who, while reading Sophocles' *Ajax* in hospital, suddenly defenestrated himself, a form of resignation that has never really caught on as it should.

At one point, Ferrell notes that Truman actually gave thought to the sufferings of women and children should we go nuclear in Korea. As for Truman's original decision to use two atomic bombs on Japan, most now agree that a single demonstration would have been quite enough to cause a Japanese surrender while making an attractive crater lake out of what had been Mount Fujiyama's peak. But Truman was in a bit of a daze at the time, as were the 13 million of us under arms who loudly applauded his abrupt ending of the first out-

and-out race war, where the Japanese had taken to castrating Marines, alive as well as dead, while Marines, good brand-name-conscious Americans, would stick Coca-Cola bottles up living Japanese soldiers and then break them off. Welcome to some *pre*-fun-house memories still vivid to ancient survivors. The story that Lieutenant R. M. Nixon tried to persuade the Marines to use Pepsi-Cola bottles has never been verified.

The climate of intimidation that began with the loyalty oath of 1947 remains with us even though two American generations have been born with no particular knowledge of what the weather was like before the great freeze and the dramatic change in our form of government. No thorough history of what actually happened to us and to the world 1945–97 has yet appeared. There are interesting glances at this or that detail. There are also far too many silly hagiographies of gallant little guy Truman and superstatesman George Marshall, who did admit to Acheson that he had no idea what on earth the plan in his name was really about. But aside from all the American and foreign dead from Korea to Vietnam, from Guatemala to the Persian Gulf, the destruction of our old republic's institutions has been the great hurt. Congress has surrendered to the executive not only the first of its great powers, but the second, the power of the purse, looks to be up for grabs as Congress is forcing more money on the Pentagon than even that black hole has asked for, obliging the executive to spend many hot hours in the vast kitchen where the books are forever being cooked in bright-red ink. As for our Ouija-board Supreme Court, it would be nice if they would take time off from holding séances with the long-dead founders, whose original intent so puzzles them, and actually examine what the founders wrought, the Constitution itself and the Bill of Rights.*

Did anyone speak out during the half-century that got us $5 trillion into debt while reducing the median household income by 7 percent when . . . No. Sorry. Too boring. Or, as Edward S. Herman writes, "Paul Krugman admits, in *Age of Diminished Expectations*, that the worsening of the income distribution was 'the central fact about economic life in America in the 1980s,' but as an issue 'it has basically exhausted the patience of the American public' "—the ten-minute attention span, unlike the green-span, has snapped on that one—"and 'no policy change now under discussion seems likely to narrow the gap significantly.' "

It was *The New Yorker*'s literary and social critic Edmund Wilson who first sounded the alarm. In 1963 he published

---

*Unfortunately, in December 2000, they took time off and hi-jacked a presidential election.

The Cold War and the Income Tax. Stupidly, he admits, he filed no income-tax returns between 1946 and 1955. As I've noted, one of the great events of our first year in the fun house was the publication in 1946 of Wilson's novel *Memoirs of Hecate County*. Wilson's income—never much—doubled. Then a system of justice, forever alert to sexual indecency, suppressed his book by court order. He was now broke with an expensively tangled marital life. Wilson describes being hounded by agents of the IRS; he also goes into the background of the federal income tax, which dates, as we know it, from 1913. Wilson also notes that, as of the 1960s, we were paying more taxes than we did during the Second World War. Since NSC-68 would remain a secret for another twelve years, he had no way of knowing that punitive income taxes must be borne by the American people in order to build up both nuclear and conventional forces to "protect" ourselves from a Second World country of, as yet, no danger to anyone except weak neighbors along its borders.

In my review of Wilson's polemic (*Book Week*, November 3, 1963) I wrote: "In public services, we lag behind all the industrialized nations of the West, preferring that the public money go not to the people but to big business. The result is a unique society in which we have free enterprise for the poor and socialism for the rich."

It should be noted—but seldom is—that the Depression did not end with the New Deal of 1933–40. In fact, it flared up again, worse than ever, in 1939 and 1940. Then, when FDR spent some $20 billion on defense (1941), the Depression was over and Lord Keynes was a hero. This relatively small injection of public money into the system reduced unemployment to 8 percent and, not unnaturally, impressed the country's postwar managers: If you want to avoid depression, spend money on war. No one told them that the same money spent on the country's infrastructure would have saved us debt, grief, blood.

What now seems to us as Wilson's rather dizzy otherworldly approach to paying taxes is, in the context of his lifetime, reasonable. In 1939, only 4 million tax returns were filed: less than 10 percent of the workforce. According to Richard Polenberg, "By the summer of 1943, nearly all Americans paid taxes out of their weekly earnings, and most were current in their payments. . . . [And thus] a foundation for the modern tax structure had been erected." Then some unsung genius thought up the withholding tax, and all the folks were well and truly locked in. Wilson knew none of this. But he had figured out the causal link between income tax and cold war:

> The truth is that the people of the United States
> are at the present time dominated and driven by

two kinds of officially propagated fear: fear of the Soviet Union and fear of the income tax. These two terrors have been adjusted so as to complement one another and thus to keep the citizen of our free society under the strain of a double pressure from which he finds himself unable to escape—like the man in the old Western story, who, chased into a narrow ravine by a buffalo, is confronted with a grizzly bear. If we fail to accept the tax, the Russian buffalo will butt and trample us, and if we try to defy the tax, the federal bear will crush us.

At the time the original North Atlantic Treaty Organization was created, only the Augustus *manqué* de Gaulle got the point to what we were doing; he took France out of our Cosa Nostra and developed his own atomic bomb. But France was still very much linked to the imperiurn. Through the CIA and other secret forces, political control was exerted within the empire, not only driving the British Labour prime minister Harold Wilson around a bend too far but preventing Italy from ever having a cohesive government by not allowing the "historic compromise"—a government of Christian Democrats and Communists—to take place. The Soviet, always reactive, promptly cracked down on their client states Czechoslovakia, Hungary, East Germany; and a wall went up in Berlin, to spite their face. From 1950 to 1990, Europe was dangerously divided; and armed to the teeth. But as American producers of weapons were never richer, all was well with their world.

At Yalta, Roosevelt wanted to break up the European colonial empires, particularly that of the French. Of Indochina he said, "France has milked it for a hundred years." For the time being, he proposed a UN trusteeship. Then he died. Unlike Roosevelt, Truman was not a philatelist. Had he been a stamp collector, he might have known where the various countries in the world were and who lived in them.

But like every good American, Truman knew he hated Communism. He also hated socialism, which may or may not have been the same thing. No one seemed quite sure. Yet as early as the American election of 1848, socialism— imported by comical German immigrants with noses always in books—was an ominous specter, calculated to derange a raw capitalist society with labor unions, health care, and other Devil's work still being fiercely resisted a century and a half later. In 1946, when Ho Chi Minh asked the United States to take Indochina under its wing, Truman said, No way. You're some kind of Fu Manchu Communist—the worst. In August 1945, Truman told de Gaulle that the French could return to Indochina: we were no longer FDR anti-imperialists. As Ho had his northern republic, the French installed Bao Dai in the South. February 1, 1950, the State Department reported, "The choice confronting the United States is to support the French in Indochina or face the extension of Communism over the remainder of the continental area of Southeast Asia and, possibly, further westward." Thus, without shepherds or even a napalm star, the domino theory was born in a humble State Department manger. On May 8, 1950, Acheson recommended economic and military aid to the French in Vietnam. By 1955, the U.S. was paying 40 percent of the French cost of war. For a quarter-century, the United States was to fight in Vietnam because our ignorant leaders and their sharp-eyed financiers never realized that the game, at best, is always chess and never dominoes.

But nothing ever stays the same. During the last days of the waning moon, a haphazard Western European economic union was cobbled together; then, as the Soviet abruptly let go its empire, the two Germanys that we had so painstakingly kept apart reunited. Washington was suddenly adrift, and in the sky the moon of empire paused. Neither Reagan nor Bush had much knowledge of history or geography. Nevertheless, orders still kept coming from

the White House. But they were less and less heeded
because everyone knows that the Oval One has a bank
overdraft of $5 trillion and he can no longer give presents
to good clients or wage war without first passing the hat to
the Germans and Japanese, as he was obliged to do when it
came time to sponsor CNN's light show in the Persian Gulf.
Gradually, it is now becoming evident to even the most dis-
tracted funster that there is no longer any need for NATO,
because there is no enemy. One might say there never really
was one when NATO was started, but, over the years, we
did succeed in creating a pretty dangerous Soviet, a fun-
house-mirror version of ourselves. Although the United
States may yet, in support of Israel, declare war on 1 billion
Muslims, the Europeans will stay out. They recall 1529,
when the Turks besieged Vienna not as obliging guest
workers but as world conquerors. Never again.

In the wake of the Madrid NATO summit, it is time for
the United States to step away from Europe—gracefully. Certainly the Europeans think it is time for us to go, as their dis-
dainful remarks at Denver betrayed, particularly when they
were warned not to walk more than a block or two from their
hotels for fear of being robbed, maimed, murdered. Yet why
do we persist in holding on to empire? *Cherchez la monnaie*,
as the clever French say. Ever since 1941, when Roosevelt got
us out of the Depression by pumping federal money into

rearming, war or the threat of war has been the principal engine to our society. Now the war is over. Or is it? Can we *afford* to give up our—well, cozy unremitting war? Why not—ah, the brilliance, the simplicity!—instead of shrinking, *expand* our phantom empire in Europe by popping everyone into NATO? No reason to have any particular enemy, though, who knows, if sufficiently goaded, Russia might again be persuaded to play Great Satan in our somewhat dusty chamber of horrors.

With an expanded NATO, our armsmakers—if not workers—are in for a bonanza. As it is, our sales of weapons were up 23 percent last year, to $11.3 billion in orders; meanwhile, restrictions on sales to Latin America are now being lifted. Chile, ever menaced by Ecuador, may soon buy as many as twenty-four American-made F-16 jet fighters. But an expanded NATO is the beauty part. Upon joining NATO, the lucky new club member is obliged to buy expensive weapons from the likes of Lockheed Martin, recently merged with Northrop Grumman. Since the new members have precarious economies—and the old ones are not exactly booming—the American taxpayer, a wan goose that lays few eggs, will have to borrow ever more money to foot the bill, which the Congressional Budget Office says should come to $125 billion over fifteen years with the U.S. paying $19 billion. Yeltsin correctly sees this as a hostile move against Russia, not to mention an expensive renewal of the Cold War, while our very own Delphic oracle, the ancient Janus-like mandarin George Kennan, has said that such an expansion could "inflame nationalistic anti-Western and militaristic tendencies in Russian opinion."

Where once we were told it was better to be dead than Red, now we will be told that it is better to be broke than— what?—slaves of the Knights of Malta? Meanwhile, conservative think tanks (their salaries paid directly or indirectly by interested conglomerates) are issuing miles of boilerplate about the necessity of securing the Free World from enemies; and Lockheed Martin lobbies individual senators, having spent (officially) $2.3 million for Congressional and presidential candidates in the 1996 election.

For those interested in just how ruinous NATO membership will be for the new members, there is the special report *NATO Expansion: Time to Reconsider*, by the British American Security Information Council and the Centre for European Security and Disarmament. Jointly published November 25, 1996, the authors regard the remilitarization of the region between Berlin and Moscow as lunacy geopolitically and disastrous economically. Hungary is now aiming at a 22 percent increase in military spending this year. The Czechs and the Poles mean to double their defense spending. The world is again at risk as our "bipartisan" rulers continue loyally to serve those who actually elect them—Lockheed Martin Northrop Grumman, Boeing, McDonnell Douglas, General Electric, Mickey Mouse, and on and on. Meanwhile, as I write, the U.S. is secretly building a new generation of nuclear weapons like the W-88 Trident missile. Cost: $4 billion a year.

There comes a moment when empires cease to exert energy and become symbolic—or existential, as we used to say back in the Forties. The current wrangling over NATO demonstrates what a quandary a symbolic empire is in when it lacks the mind, much less the resources, to impose its hegemony upon former client states. At the end, entropy gets us all. Fun house falls down. Fairground's a parking lot. "So I awoke, and behold it was a dream." *Pilgrim's Progress* again. But not quite yet.

It is a truism that generals are always ready to fight the last war. The anachronistic rhetoric at Madrid in July, if ever acted upon, would certainly bring on the next—last?—big war, if only because, in Francis Bacon's words, "Upon the breaking and shivering of a great state and empire, you may be sure to have wars."

Happily, in the absence of money and common will nothing much will probably happen. Meanwhile, there is a new better world ready to be born. The optimum economic unit in the world is now the city-state. Thanks to technology, everyone knows or can know something about everyone else on the planet. The message now pounding over the Internet is the irrelevancy, not to mention sheer danger, of the traditional nation-state, much less empire. Despite currency confusions, Southeast Asia leads the way while the warlords at Peking not only are tolerating vigorous industrial semi-autonomies like Shanghai but also may have an ongoing paradigm in Hong Kong. We do not like the way Singapore is run (hardly our business), but it is, relatively speaking, a greater commercial success than the United States, which might prosper, once the empire's put out of its misery, in smaller units on the Swiss cantonal model: Spanish-speaking Catholic regions, Asian Confucian regions, consensually united mixed regions with, here and there, city-states like New York–Boston or Silicon Valley.

In the next century, barring accident, the common market in Europe will evolve not so much into a union of ancient bloodstained states as a mosaic of homogenous regions and city-states like Milan, say, each loosely linked in trade with a clearinghouse information center at Brussels to orchestrate finance and trade and the policing of cartels. Basques, Bretons, Walloons, Scots who want to be rid of onerous nation-states should be let go in order to pursue and even—why not?—overtake happiness, the goal, or so we Americans have always pretended to believe, of the human enterprise.

On that predictably sententious American note, O movers and shakers of the month, let us return to "the wilderness of this world," recalling the Hippocratic oath, which enjoins doctors: "Above all do no harm." Hippocrates also wrote, O moved and shaken, "Life is short, but the art is long, the opportunity fleeting, the experiment perilous, the judgment difficult."

Vanity Fair
November 1997

In the Lair of the Octopus

In "Murder as Policy" (April 24), Allan Nairn notes, accurately, that the "real role . . . of all U.S. ambassadors [to Guatemala] since 1954 [has been] to cover for and, in many ways, facilitate American support for a killer army." Nairn's report on the capers of one Thomas Stroock, a recent viceroy, is just another horror story in a long sequence which it was my . . . privilege? to see begin not in 1954 but even earlier, in 1946, when, at twenty, a first novel just published, I headed south of the border, ending up in Antigua, Guatemala, where I bought a ruined convent for $2,000 (the convent had been ruined, let me say in all fairness, by earthquake and not by the Guatemalan military or even by the U.S. embassy).

Guatemala was beginning to flourish. The old dictator, Ubico, an American client, had been driven out. A philosophy professor named Arévalo had been elected President in a free election. A democratic socialist or social democrat or whatever, he had brought young people into government, tamed the army, and behaved tactfully with the largest employer in the country, the American company United Fruit.

Easily the most interesting person in—and out—of the town was Mario Monteforte Toledo. Under thirty, he was a thin, energetic intellectual who wrote poetry. He had a wife in the capital and an Indian girlfriend in Antigua, and when he came to visit, he and I would meet and talk, and talk.

Mario was President of the Guatemalan Congress and was regarded by everyone as a future President of the republic. In politics he was vaguely socialist. I, of course, reflecting my family's politics, was fiercely Tory. We had splendid rows.

Scene: patio of my house. Overhanging it the high wall of the adjacent church of El Carmen. Under a pepper tree, near an ugly square fountain like a horse trough, we would sit and drink beer. He told me the gossip. Then, after a ritual denunciation of the rich and the indifferent, Mario started to talk politics. "We may not last much longer."

"We . . . who?"

"Our government. At some point we're going to have to raise revenue. The only place where there is any money to be raised is *el pulpo*." *El pulpo* meant the Octopus, also known as the United Fruit Company, whose annual revenues were twice that of the Guatemalan state. Recently workers had gone on strike; selfishly, they had wanted to be paid $1.50 a day for their interesting work.

"What's going to stop you from taxing them?" I was naïve. This was long ago and the United States had just become the Leader of the Lucky Free World.

"Your government. Who else? They kept Ubico in power all those years. Now they're getting ready to replace us."

I was astonished. I had known vaguely about our numerous past interventions in Central America. But that was past. Why should we bother now? We controlled most of the world. "Why should we care what happens in a small country like this?"

Mario gave me a compassionate look—compassion for my stupidity. "Businessmen. Like the owners of United Fruit. They care. They used to pay for our politicians. They still pay for yours. Why, one of your big senators is on the board of *el pulpo*."

I knew something about senators. Which one? Mario was vague. "He has three names. He's from Boston, I think. . . ."

"Henry Cabot Lodge? I don't believe it." Lodge was a family friend; as a boy I had discussed poetry with him—he was a poet's son. Years later, as Kennedy's Ambassador to Vietnam, he would preside over the murder of the Diem brothers.

As we drank beer and the light faded, Mario described
the trap that a small country like Guatemala was in. I can't
say that I took him very seriously. With all the world,
except the satanic Soviet Union, under our control it was
hardly in our national interest to overthrow a democratic
neighbor, no matter how much its government irritated the
board of directors of United Fruit. But in those days I was
not aware to what extent big business controlled the government of our own rapidly expiring Republic. Now, of
course, everyone knows to what extent our subsequent
empire, with its militarized economy, controls business.
The end result is much the same for the rest of the world,
only the killing fields are more vast than before and we
make mischief not just with weak neighbors but on every
continent.

Mario had given me the idea for a novel. A dictator (like
Ubico) returns from an American exile as the Octopus's
candidate to regain power. I would tell the story through
the eyes of a young American war veteran (like myself) who
joins the general out of friendship for his son. The more I
brooded on the story, the more complexities were revealed.
Dark Green, Bright Red. The Greens, father and son, were the
Company, and dark figures indeed, haunting the green jun-
gles. Bright Red was not only blood but the possibility of a
communist taking power.

"No novel about—or from—Latin America has ever been a success in English." As of 1950, my publisher was right.

Four years after the book was published, Senator Lodge denounced Arévalo's popularly elected successor, Arbenz, as a communist because, in June 1952, Arévalo had ordered the expropriation of some of United Fruit's unused land, which he gave to 100,000 Guatemalan families. Arévalo paid the company what he thought was a fair price, their own evaluation of the land for tax purposes. The American Empire went into action, and through the CIA, it put together an army and bombed Guatemala City. U.S. Ambassador John Peurifoy behaved rather like Mr. Green in the novel. Arbenz resigned. Peurifoy wanted the Guatemalan army's chief of staff to become President, and gave him a list of "communists" to be shot. The chief of staff declined: "It would be better," he said, "that *you* actually sit in the presidential chair and that the Stars and Stripes fly over the palace."

Puerifoy picked another military man to represent the interests of company and empire. Since then, Guatemala has been a slaughterground, very bright red indeed against the darkest imperial green. Later, it was discovered that Arbenz had no communist connections, but the "disinformation" had been so thorough that few Americans knew to what extent they had been lied to by a government that had now put itself above law and, rather worse, beyond reason.

Incidentally, I note that the disinformation still goes on. In the April 9 *New York Times* (a "recovering" newspaper in recent years), one Clifford Krauss airily says that Guatemala's Indians have been regularly screwed for four hundred years, so what else is new? He gives a tendentious history of the country—purest Langley boilerplate, circa 1955—but omits the crucial 1931–44 dictatorship of Jorge Ubico.

I must say I find it disconcerting to read in 1995 that "by surrounding himself with Communist Party advisers, accepting arms from Czechoslovakia and building a port to compete with United Fruit's facilities, Arbenz challenged the United States at the height of the cold war." God, to think that such evil ever walked the Central American night! "President Eisenhower's CIA organized a Guatemalan [*sic*] invasion force and bombed Guatemala City in 1954."

Dark Green, Bright Red was just reissued in England. Reviewing it in the *Evening Standard*, the journalist Patrick Skene Catling writes, "I wish I had read this prophetic work of fiction before my first visit to Guatemala in 1954. Gore Vidal would have helped me to understand how John Peurifoy . . . was able to take me up to the roof of his embassy to watch . . . the air raids without anxiety, because he and the CIA knew exactly where the bombs were going to fall.

A final note—of bemusement, I suppose. I was at school with Nathaniel Davis, who was our ambassador in Chile at the time of Allende's overthrow. A couple of years later Davis was Ambassador to Switzerland and we had lunch at the Berne embassy. I expressed outrage at our country's role in the matter of Chile. Davis "explained" *his* role. Then he asked, "Do you take the line that the United States should never intervene in the affairs of another country?" I said that unless an invasion was being mounted against us in Mexico, no, we should never intervene. Davis, a thoughtful man, thought; then he said, "Well, it would be nice in diplomacy, or in life, if one could ever start from a point of innocence." To which I suppose the only answer is to say— Go! Plunge ever deeper, commit more crimes to erase those already committed, and repeat with Macbeth, "I am in blood / Stepped in so far that, should I wade no more, / Returning were as tedious as go o'er."

The Nation
June 5, 1995

MICKEY MOUSE, HISTORIAN

On June 3, 1996, *The Nation* showed in a foldout chart how most of the U.S. media are now owned by a handful of corporations. Several attractive octopi decorated the usually chaste pages of this journal. The most impressive of these cephalopod molluscs was that headed by Disney-ABC, taking precedence over the lesser Time Warner, General Electric–NBC, and Westinghouse Corporation calamari, from which dangle innumerable tentacles representing television (network and cable), weapons factories (GE aircraft engines and nuclear turbines) and, of course, GNA and other insurance firms unfriendly to health care reform.

As I studied this beast, I felt a bit like Rip Van Winkle. When last I nodded off, there was something called the Sherman Antitrust Act. Whatever happened to it? How can any octopus control so much opinion without some objection from . . . from whom? That's the problem. Most mem-

bers of Congress represent not states or people but corporations—and octopi. Had I simply dreamed John Sherman?
Or had he been devoured by Dragon Synergy? Little did I
suspect, as I sighed over this latest demonstration of how
tightly censored we are by the few, that, presently, I would
be caught in the tentacles of the great molluscs Disney-ABC
and General Electric–NBC, as well as the Hearst Corporation, whose jointly owned cable enterprise Arts & Enter-
tainment had spawned, in 1995, something called The
History Channel.

"It all began in the cold," as Arthur Schlesinger so
famously began his romantic historical novel *A Thousand
Days*. Only my cold was London, where, for Channel Four,
I wrote and narrated three half-hour programs on the
American presidency, emphasizing the imperial aspects
latent in the office from the beginning, and ending, currently, with our uneasy boast that we are the last great
global power on the . . . well, globe.

The programs were well received in Britain. The History
Channel bought the U.S. rights. In ninety-minute form,
my view of the imperial presidency was to be shown just
before the 1996 political conventions. But then, from the
tiny tentacle tip of The History Channel, synergy began to
surge up the ownership arm, through NBC to its longtime

master General Electric; then ever upward, to, presumably, the supreme mollusc, Mickey Mouse himself, Lord of Anaheim. *Great Mouse, this program attacks General Electric by name. Attacks American imperialism, which doesn't exist. Bad-mouths all that we hold sacred.* Oh, to have been a fly on the castle wall when word arrived! The easy solution, as Anaheim's hero-president, R. M. Nixon, might have said, would have been to kill the program. But craftier minds were at work. *We'll get some "experts" like we do for those crappy historical movies and let them take care of this Commie.*

So it came to pass that, unknown to me, a GE panel was assembled; it comprised two flyweight journalists from television's Jurassic Age (Roger Mudd, Sander Vanocur) and two professors, sure to be hostile (one was my old friend Arthur Schlesinger, about whose client, JFK, I am unkind; the other was someone called Richard Slotkin). I was not invited to defend myself, nor was anyone else. As a spokesperson for The History Channel put it, "Vidal is so *opinionated* that we had to have real experts on." *The Nation*'s recent warning about the danger of allowing the corporate few to make and control mass opinion was about to be dramatized at my expense.

Fade in: Roger Mudd. He is grim. He wears, as it were, not so much the black cap of the hanging judge as the symbol of his awful power, *Mickey Mouse ears.* He describes my

career with distaste. Weirdly, he says I had "social ambitions at the Kennedy White House and [*non sequitur*] ran for
Congress" but lost. Actually, I ran for Congress before
Kennedy got to the White House. Also, in upstate New
York, I got some twenty thousand more votes than JFK did
as head of the ticket. During my campaign, Bobby Kennedy
came to see me at Saugerties Landing. It was, appropriately,
Halloween. "Why," he snarled, "don't you ever mention
the ticket?" "Because I want to win," I said, imitating his
awful accent. That started the feud.

Mudd reports that I am "acerbic, acid-tongued," don't
live in the United States (except when I do), and the viewer
is warned beforehand that this is only my "bilious look" at
American history and our presidents, whom Mudd says
that I describe variously as incompetent, avaricious war-
mongers. This is—warmongering to one side—slanderously
untrue. Then, Mickey Mouse ears atremble with righteous
indignation, he reassures us that, at program's end, *real* historians will set the record straight. And so, muddied but
unbowed, I fade in.

I begin in a sort of mock-up of the White House TV room.
I say a few mildly bilious words about current politics:

> He who can raise the most money to buy time
>   on television is apt to be elected President by

that half of the electorate that bothers to vote. Since the same corporations pay for our two-party, one-party system, there is little or no actual politics in these elections. But we do get a lot of sex. Also, he who subtly hates the blacks the most will always win a plurality of the lily-white-hearted. The word "liberal" has been totally demonized, while "conservative," the condition of most income-challenged Americans, is being tarnished by godly pressure groups whose symbols are the fetus and the flag. As a result, today's candidates are now rushing toward a meaningless place called "the center," and he who can get to the center of the center—the dead center, as it were—will have a four-year lease on this studio.

I then trace the history of our expansionist presidents from Jefferson's Louisiana Purchase to Bush of Mesopotamia's Gulf War, produced by Ted Turner's CNN, a sort of in-house TV war. I end the program in front of the Vietnam Memorial. We have come a long way, I say, from Jefferson's Declaration of Independence to "the skies over Baghdad have been illuminated." Then Mudd, more than ever horrified by what he'd seen and heard,

introduces a TV journalist called Vanocur, who introduces Professors Schlesinger and Slotkin. It's very clear,
says Vanocur, that Vidal doesn't like America. Arthur's
response is mild. Well, let's say he is disappointed in
what's happened.

At the beginning of Mudd's first harangue, I must say I
did wonder what on earth had caused such distress. It was
clear that neither cue-card reader had any particular
interest—much less competence—in American history; but
then, I had forgotten the following aria:

> Our presidents, now prisoners of security, have
> been for a generation, two-dimensional figures
> on a screen. In a sense, captives of the empire
> they created. Essentially, they are men hired to
> give the commercials for a state which more and
> more resembles a conglomerate like General
> Electric. In fact, one of our most popular recent
> presidents spent nearly twenty years actually
> doing commercials for General Electric, one of
> our greatest makers of weapons. Then Mr.
> Reagan came to work here [in the White House],
> and there was the same "Russians are coming"
> dialogue on the same TelePrompTer, and the
> same makeup men.

The GE panel, carefully, made no reference to their fellow pitchman Reagan, but they found unbearable my suggestion that we have been surpassed, economically, by Asia. I noted that:

> As Japan takes its turn as a world leader, *temporarily standing in for China,** America becomes the Yellow Man's Burden, and so we come full circle. Europe began as the relatively empty, uncivilized Wild West of Asia. Then the Americas became the Wild West of Europe. Now the sun, setting in our West, is rising once more in the East.

This really hurt Mudd, and he couldn't resist noting that Japan's standard of living is lower than ours, a factoid that, presumably, magically cancels our vast debt to them. He reminds us that we have also been hearing a lot of bad economic news about other countries; but then we always do, lest Americans ever feel that they are being shortchanged by a government that gives its citizens nothing for their tax money and companies like General Electric billions for often-useless weapons and cost overruns. Approvingly,

*Italics added for 2000.

Mudd tells us that "industrious immigrants" are rushing to our shores. Well, those we have helped to impoverish south of the Rio Grande do come looking for work, particularly from countries whose societies we have wrecked in the name, often, of corporate America (United Fruit in Guatemala, ITT in Chile), or they come from Southern Asia, where our interferences dislocated millions of people, some of whom unwisely boated to our shores, lured by our generous minimum wage, universal health care, and superb state educational system.

Mudd's mouse squeak becomes very grave indeed as he tells us how the defense budget has been slashed to a mere fraction of what it used to be and must be increased if we are ever to keep the peace of the world through war. Yet today we outspend the military budgets of Western Europe and Japan combined. Although there have been large cuts in personnel as military bases are turned over to the real estate lobby, outlays of the sort that benefit Mudd's employers still run to nearly $300 billion a year.

The two historians were less openly protective of General Electric and military procurement. Schlesinger doesn't find much in the way of historical distortion. But then, what motive would I have had to neglect what Jefferson liked to call "true facts"? I am neither political publicist nor hagiographer, and I know the country's history as well as most people who have dedicated a generation to its study.

Schlesinger does say that I misquote Jefferson's Declaration of Independence. That must sound pretty serious to the average viewer. It also sounds pretty serious to me that Arthur doesn't realize I was quoting, accurately, the original preamble, not the one edited and published by Congress. Jefferson—and I—preferred his first version, of which only a fragment still exists but, luckily, later in life he re-created the original: "All men are created equal and independent." Congress cut the "and independent." Then: "From that equal creation, they derive rights inherent and inalienable." Congress (looking ahead to the Rev. Pat Robertson and all the other serpents in our Eden?) changed this to "They are endowed by their Creator with certain inalienable rights." The introduction of a Creator has done our independence no good.

Early on, I observe that "an adviser to President Truman announced, 'What is good for General Motors is good for America.' The adviser was president of General Motors, of course." Arthur correctly notes that Charles Wilson was not a member of Truman's Cabinet but of Eisenhower's. Nevertheless, he was a significant *adviser* to Truman. Unfortunately, his famous advice to Truman got edited out of my final program. Here it is. In 1944 Wilson gave his rationale for a permanent militarizing of the economy: "Instead of looking to disarmament and unpreparedness as a safeguard against war—a thoroughly discredited doctrine—let us try the opposite: full preparedness according to a continuing plan." This was to be the heart of the National Security Act of 1947, and the new nation in whose shabby confines we still rattle about.

It is a little late in the day to turn Lincoln into an abolitionist, but the GE panel saw an easy way of making points by piously declaring how much great-hearted Lincoln hated slavery. But I had already noted, "He disliked slavery but thought the federal government had no right to free other people's property. In this case, three million African-Americans at the South." It should be noted—yet again—that American history departments are now bustling with propagandists revising Lincoln so that he will appear to be something quite other than the man who said that if he could preserve the Union by freeing all the slaves, he would do so; or freeing some and not others, he would do so; or freeing none at all, he would free none for the Union's sake. But for General Electric, blushing bride of Mickey Mouse, the image of Lincoln cannot remain half Disney and half true.

At one point, Slotkin accuses me of dealing in hindsight. But that, dear professor, is what history is, and you and I and even Arthur are historians, aren't we? It is true that I refused election to the Society of American Historians; but I am no less a historian than those who are paid to keep the two essential facts of our condition from the people at large: the American class system (there is no such thing, we are flatly told) and the nature of the U.S. empire (no such thing, either). Apparently, it is perfectly natural for a freedom-loving democracy, addicted to elections, to have bases and spies and now FBI terrorist fighters and drug hounds in every country on earth. When Vanocur tries to get Theodore Roosevelt off the imperialist hook, Schlesinger does mutter that the great warmonger did believe in "a vigorous foreign policy." Then Arthur makes a slip: TR was really only interested in our "domination of the Western Hemisphere." Well, certainly half a globe is better than none. But then, as TR said, "No accomplishment of peace is half that of the glories of war."

Schlesinger notes that if Jefferson and John Quincy Adams were to return today, they would be surprised that we had not annexed Canada, Cuba, and other Western properties. For the GE panel, such continence is proof that there is no such thing as a U.S. empire. Well, it is true that after two failed invasions, Canada escaped us; even so, we have a naval base on Canadian soil (at Argentia), and Canada plays its dutiful if irritable part in our imperium, economically as well as militarily. Cuba was, in effect, our brothel during the Batista years; now, for trying to be independent of us, it is embargoed while we maintain on the island, as always, the military base of Guantanamo.

Toward the end of their "discussion," one of the Mouseketeers mocks the notion that big business is in any way responsible for a U.S. empire that does not exist. The GE panel, to a man, then proceeds to ignore this key section of my script:

> TR's successor, Woodrow Wilson, invaded Mexico
> and Haiti in order to bring those poor people
> freedom and democracy and good government.
> But stripped of all the presidential rhetoric, the
> flag followed the banks.
>
> The President was simply chief enforcer for
> the great financial interests.
>
> Many years later, the commanding general of
> the U.S. Marine Corps, General Smedley Butler,
> blew, as it were, the whistle, not just on Wilson,
> but on the whole imperial racket.

I had showed some fine newsreel footage of Butler, of Marines in Haiti, Taiwan, the streets of Shanghai. I did an imitation of his voice as I spoke his actual words:

> "I spent most of my time being a high-class

muscle man for big business, for Wall Street and
for the bankers. In short, I was a racketeer, a
gangster for capitalism. I helped make Mexico
safe for American oil interests in 1914. Made in
Haiti and Cuba a decent place for the National
City Bank boys to collect revenues in."

In later years, Butler also set up shop in Nicaragua, the
Dominican Republic, and China where, it 1927, the
Marines protected Standard Oil's interests.

Vidal as Butler: "The best Al Capone had was
three districts. I operated on three continents."

Needless to say, General Butler is a permanent nonfigure
in our imperial story.

Slotkin began to paraphrase exactly what I had been
saying—modern empires are not like the old-fashioned sort
where you raise your flag over the capitol of a foreign
country. From 1950 on, I demonstrated how the domination of other countries is exercised through the economy
(the Marshall Plan after World War II) and through a military presence, preferably low-key (like NATO in Western
Europe) and politically through secret police like the CIA,
the FBI, the DEA, the DIA, etc. Currently, the empire is

ordering its vassal states not to deal with rogue nations (the Helms-Burton bill).

Although the Soviet Union went out of business five years ago, we still have bases in Belgium, Germany, Greece, Italy, the Netherlands, Portugal, Spain, Turkey. In Britain we have seven air force and three naval bases. In 1948, Secretary of Defense Forrestal installed two B-29 groups in the English countryside; it would be a good idea, he said, to accustom the English to a continuing U.S. military presence. To create and administer a modern empire, you must first discover—or invent—a common enemy and then bring all the potential victims of this ogre under *your* domination, using your secret services to skew their politics as the CIA did, say, to Harold Wilson's Labour Party.

Today, elsewhere, we have military presences in Bermuda, Egypt, Iceland, Japan, Korea, Panama, the Philippines, Saudi Arabia, Kuwait, etc., not to mention all over the United States and our territories as well as two bases in Australia, one of which is a mysterious CIA unit at Alice Springs. If all this does not constitute an empire, I don't know what does. Yet we must not use the word, for reasons that the GE panel never addressed. At one point, Vanocur pretended that I had said the American people were eager for conquest when I said the opposite. Our people tend to isolationism and it always takes a lot of corporate manipulation, as well as imperial presidential mischief, to get them into foreign wars. Sadly, Schlesinger confirmed that this was so.

Slotkin thought that I had been saying that the late-nineteenth-century presidents were creatures of big business when what I said was that big business was off on its rampage and that the presidents, between Lincoln and Theodore Roosevelt, were dimly accommodating.

Then the question of why I was so evil was gravely addressed. Mouse ears were now on the alert. Schlesinger noted that I had headed the America First chapter at Exeter in 1940 and that I still seemed to be an isolationist. Vanocur said isolationists were right-wingers. Schlesinger countered that many, like Norman Thomas (and me), were on the left. Mud, as it were, in hand, Vanocur said that isolationism is "tinged with anti-Semitism," but that did not play. Schlesinger did note, with a degree of wonder, that there are those who do not seem to understand how our future is inextricably bound up in the politics of all the other continents. This might have been a good place to start an enlightening debate. Had I been included, I might have said that unless the nation is in actual peril (or in need of loot—I am not angelic) there is never any reason for us to engage in foreign wars. Since George Washington, the isolationist has always had the best arguments. But since

corporate money is forever on the side of foreign adventure, money has kept us on the move, at least until recently.

I said that Stalin drastically disarmed after the war.
Arthur rightly pointed out that so did we: pressure from the
isolationist masses forced the government to let go millions
of GIs, including me. But two days after the announcement
of Japan's surrender, Truman said (August 17, 1945) that he
would ask Congress to approve a program of universal military training—in peacetime! He made the request, and got
his wish. We rearmed as they disarmed. Briefly.

Between May and September 1946, Truman began the
rearmament of our sector of Germany while encouraging
the French in their recolonization of Indochina, as well as
meddling militarily in China and South Korea. The great
problem of living in a country where information and education are so tightly controlled is that very little news about
our actual situation ever gets through to the consumers.
Instead we are assured that we are so hated by those
envious of our wealth and goodness that they commit terrorist acts against us simply out of spite. The damage our
presidential and corporate imperialists have done to others
in every quarter of the world is a nonsubject, as we saw in
August, when my realistic overview accidentally appeared
on an imperial network and a panel of four was rushed into
place to glue mouse ears back on the eagle's head.

Vanocur then affects to be mystified by why I say so many terrible things about the Disneyland that pays him his small salary. But I thought I had made myself clear. I am a patriot of the old Republic that slowly unraveled during the expansionist years and quite vanished in 1950 when the National Security State took its place. Now I want us to convert from a wartime to a peacetime economy. But since the GE-style conglomerates that govern us will never convert, something will have to give, won't it?

When the egregious Vanocur wondered why I had done this program, Arthur said, "To entertain himself—and to entertain the audience." That was disappointing, but worthy of the Dr. Faustus of Harvard Yard.

I did not report on my country's disastrous imperial activities with much amusement. All I wanted to do was tell a story never told before on our television—and never to be told again as long as the likes of GE and Disney are allowed to be media owners and manipulators of opinion.

What to do? Break up the conglomerates. That's a start. And then—well, why not go whole hog—what about a free press, representative government and . . . Well, you get the picture.

The Nation
September 30, 1996

III

WITH EXTREME PREJUDICE

rticle I, Section 9 of the Constitution requires government agencies to submit their budgets at regular intervals to Congress for review. Neither the CIA nor the DIA does this.* Occasionally, at the dark of the moon, they will send someone up to the Hill to disinform Congress, and that's that. After all, to explain what they actually do with the money that they get would be a breach of national security, the overall rubric that protects so many of them from criminal indictments. Although most Americans now think that the CIA was created at Valley Forge by General Washington, this unaccountable spy service was invented less than half a century ago, and since that time we have been systematically misinformed about the rest of the world for domestic policy reasons (remember Russia's outstanding economic surge in 1980?). Intelligence

*Central Intelligence Agency, Defense Intelligence Agency.

is an empty concept unless directly related to action. In a war, knowledge of the enemy's troop movements is all-important. In peacetime, random intelligence-gathering is meaningless, when not sinister.

Since our rulers have figured that one out, they have done their best to make sure that we shall never be at peace; hence, the necessity of tracking enemies—mostly imaginary ones, as the Pentagon recently revealed in its wonderfully wild scenarios for future wars. Since Communism's ultimate crime against humanity was to go out of business, we now have no universal war to conduct except the one against drugs (more than $20 billion was wasted last year on this crusade). As there is now no longer sufficient money for any of these "wars," there is no longer a rationale for so many secret services unless the Feds really come out of the closet and declare war on the American people, the ultimate solution: after all, one contingency plan in Ollie North's notebook suggested that in a time of crisis, dusky-hued Americans should be sequestered.

I would suggest that the State Department return to its once-useful if dull task of supplying us with information about other countries so that we might know more about what they'd like to buy from us. The hysterical tracking down of nuclear weapons is useless. After all, we, or our treasured allies, have armed all the world to the teeth. We have neither the money nor the brains to monitor every country on earth, which means, alas, that if some evil dictator in Madagascar wants to nuke or biologically degrade Washington, D.C., there's not much we can do about it. Certainly, the CIA, as now constituted, would be the last to know of his intention, though perhaps the first to get the good of his foul plot. I would abandon all the military-related secret services and I would keep the FBI on a tight leash—no more dirty tricks against those who dislike the way that we are governed, and no more dossiers on those of us who might be able to find a way out of the mess we are in, best personified by the late J. Edgar Hoover and best memorialized by that Pennsylvania Avenue Babylonian fortress that still bears his infamous name.

The Nation
June 8, 1992

The Union of the State

Over the years I have written quite a lot about the state of the Union. Now, in the interest of novelty, I'd like to discuss the *Union* of the State. I have always tried to say something so obvious that no one else has noticed it. For instance, I once suggested that we criminalize most firearms, and legalize most drugs. This would put an end to the now-eternal War on Crime that, we are told, is devastating our alabaster cities and not doing the amber waves of marijuana much good either. I realize, of course, that vested interests are now too great for us to do anything of an intelligent nature in this—or almost any—regard. The National Rifle Association will never wither away as long as there is a single Congressman left to be paid off or a child unarmed.

Our violence and murder rate are unique in the First World. This may be a negative uniqueness but it is all our own, and to be cherished; at least we are number one at something other than indebtedness. We now have over a million people in prison* and another couple of million on probation or parole; why not just lock up half the population and force the other half to guard them? That would solve crime; it might also entice Amnesty International to start whining here at home. After all, 58 percent of those in our federal prisons are there for drug offenses. Most are not dangerous to the public, and even though our overkindly government thinks they are dangerous to themselves, they should still be allowed to pursue their constitutional, if unhealthful, happiness in freedom. Certainly they do not deserve to be confined to a prison system that a Scandinavian commission recently reported to be barbarous for a supposedly First World country.

Unfortunately, the rulers of *any* system cannot maintain their power without the constant creation of prohibitions that then give the state the right to imprison—or otherwise intimidate—anyone who violates any of the state's often new-minted crimes. Without communism—once monolithic and on the march—our state lacks a Wizard of Oz to terrify all the people all the time. So the state looks inward,

---

*As of 2000, USA Today *reports on its front page that 6.6 million adults (3 percent of the adult population) are in prison or "correction." No other society has ever done so deadly a thing to its people and on such a scale.*

at the true enemy, who turns out to be—who else? the people of the United States. In the name of correctness, of good health, or even of God—a great harassment of the people-at-large is now going on. Although our state has not the power to intimidate any but small, weak countries, we can certainly throw most Americans in prison for violating the ever-increasing list of prohibitions. Will this change for the better with a change of Congress or President? No. Things are going to get a lot worse until we apply the state's new white hope to the state itself: Three strikes, you're out. How then to "strike out" the state? I have an idea.

Kevin Phillips recently attacked—in *Time*—Washington, D.C., a beautiful city, built, if not on a hill, at least on what, in 1800, was a quite attractive swamp. He quoted Jefferson's warning that when every aspect of government is drawn to Washington—he meant the city, not the general—Washington, in his words, would become "as venal and oppressive as the government from which we separated." (This was England, by the way, not the Disney studio so recently and bloodily thrown back at Bull Run.)

Phillips tacitly acknowledges that the people have no representation within the Beltway, unlike the banks or insurance companies. Consequently, officeholders and their shadow, the media, are equally disliked by a vast majority. Unfortunately, the people are without alternative.

That is what makes the situation so volatile and potentially dangerous. Think what might have happened had Ross Perot possessed the oily charm of Charlton Heston. Certainly, it is plain that when a people comes to detest the political system in which it is entrapped, that system will not endure for long.

I've always been mystified at how obtuse politicians and the media are. Every politician of consequence, for the last quarter-century, has run against Washington, against lobbyists, against insiders, against Jefferson's "venal and oppressive" ruling class—or, to be precise, the representatives of our actual rulers, who circle the globe like Puck with all the swift anonymous speed of a fax laden with campaign money. It is very hard, one would think, to live with so total a contradiction. For instance, both Carter and Reagan campaigned against Washington, and both won. Neither understood why people voted for him. Neither made the slightest attempt, even cosmetically, to curb Jefferson's tyrannous capital. The two new employees forgot their speeches and went right on doing business as instructed by those huge economic forces that govern earth.

Can someone like Clinton make a change? I don't see how. We would like health care of the sort every civilized nation has but we can never have a rational system as long as insurance companies are allowed to benefit. The people may want affordable health care, but they are not going to get it in the United States of America as now constituted.

Phillips has come up with an old notion of mine: devolution, the dictionary word for breaking up the Union into smaller, more manageable units. He would move much of the government away from Washington, I suppose to inconvenience the 800,000 lawyers who will then be able to deduct as legitimate travel expense the weary weekly journey from cozy Montgomery County to sky-topped Denver. He would move various departments permanently to other states and rotate the capital from this to that city. He would like an amendment to the Constitution "setting up a mechanism for holding nationwide referendums to permit the citizenry to supplant Congress and the President in making certain categories of national decisions." Like declarations of war? Could he be *that* radical? Along with this bit of major surgery on the body politic, he has some useful Band-Aids. But no more. Nevertheless, I am well pleased that what I've been proposing for so long has now gone mainline. So let me go a bit further out.

In 1992 I switched on CNN and heard Jerry Brown—in New Hampshire—giving pretty much a speech that I had given for the National Press Club on how to restore power to its only legitimate source, We the People. As Jerry and I had not spoken since I ran against him in the California Senate primary in 1982, I was pleasantly surprised and praised him publicly for his wisdom, while blessing him for his plagiarism, no matter how belated. He rang me in Italy. Yes, it was my speech. Unlike Joe Biden, he is an honest man. And did I have anything more? And would I come to New Hampshire? I said, yes, I had more, but, no, I would forgo the winter wonderland of New Hampshire, currently known as Dole Land.

However, thanks to CNN and the fax machine, I could monitor his campaign and send him my thoughts immediately. So a number of suggestions of mine entered the primary campaign. The principal notion was conversion from war to peace. Find a defense plant that's closing and say that it should be kept open but converted to peacetime, using the same workforce and technology. Brown did just that in Connecticut. He told the soon-to-be-dismissed makers of Seawolf submarines that if he became President, they would be making not submarines but bullet trains. At five in the morning I got a call from political operator Pat Caddell. "We won!" he said. "We won Connecticut." Then they—not we—lost New York.

Meanwhile, Perot grabbed my *We the People* as the strange device for his eccentric banner. I felt very odd, watching CNN in Italy, and hearing at least three candidates using my lines.

Jerry was headed for Pennsylvania after New York and, as the game was up, I said why not propose something really useful: launch a new idea that might take a few years to penetrate but when it does, might save us all.

Here is the gist of what I wrote him. I started with the eternal problem of what we do about income tax. As the people at large get nothing much back from the money that they give the government—Social Security is not federal income—why not just eliminate the federal income tax? How? Eliminate Washington, D.C. Allow the states and municipalities to keep what revenue they can raise. I know that tens if not hundreds of thousands of lobbyist-lawyers and hired media gurus will have a million objections. But let us pursue the notion.

Why not divide the country into several reasonably homogeneous sections, more or less on the Swiss cantonal system. Each region would tax its citizens and then provide the services those citizens wanted, particularly education and health. Washington would then become a ceremonial capital with certain functions. We shall always need some sort of modest defense system, a common currency, and a Supreme Court to adjudicate between the regions as well as to maintain the Bill of Rights—a novelty for the present Court.

How to pay for what's left of Washington? Each region will make its own treaty with the central government and send what it feels should be spent on painting the White House and on our common defense, which will, for lack of money, cease to be what it is now—all-out offense on everyone on earth. The result will be no money to waste either on pork or on those imperial pretensions that have left us $4.7 trillion in debt. Wasteful, venal, tyrannous Washington will be no more than a federal theme park administered by Michael Eisner.

Will the regions be corrupt, venal, etc.? Of course they will—we are Americans!—but they will be corrupt on an infinitesimal scale. Also, more to the point, in a smaller polity, everyone knows who's up to no good and they can police themselves better than the federal government ever could—even if it had ever wanted to.

All over the world today, centrifugal forces are at work. In a bloody war in the old Yugoslavia and parts of the old Soviet Union, and in a peaceful way in the old Czechoslovakia. Since history is nothing but the story of the migration of tribes, we must now note that the tribes are very much on the move again, and thanks to modern technology we can actually watch Bengals and Indians overflowing each other's borders.

Racially, the composition of Europe has changed more in the past fifty years than in the previous five hundred. Whether this is good or bad is irrelevant. It is. Now, here at home, people fret about invasions from the Hispanic world, from Haiti, from the boat people of Asia. But, like it or not, we are changing from a white, Protestant country, governed by males, to a mixed polity, and in this time of change there is bound to be conflict. The fragmentations that we see everywhere are the result of a *dislike* for the nation-state as we have known it since the bloody nation-building of Bismarck and Lincoln.

People want to be rid of arbitrary capitals and faraway rulers. So let the people go. If our southern tier is to be Spanish and Catholic, let it be. But also, simultaneously, as we see in Europe, while this centrifugal force is at work—a rushing away from the center—there is also a centripetal one, a coming-together of small polities in order to have better trade, defense, culture—so we are back, if by chance, to our original Articles of Confederation, a group of loosely confederated states rather than a *United* States, which has proved to be every bit as unwieldy and ultimately tyrannous as Jefferson warned. After all, to make so many of Many into only One of one you must use force, and this is a bad thing, as we experienced in the Civil War. So let us make new arrangements to conform with new realities.

I will not go so far as to say that we shall ever see anything like democracy at work in our section of North America—

traditionally we have always been a republic entirely governed by money, but at least, within the regions, there will be more diversity than there is now and, best of all, the people will at last have the sensation that they are no longer victims of a far-off government but that they—and their tax money—are home at last.

The Nation
December 26, 1994

THE LAST DEFENDER OF THE AMERICAN REPUBLIC?

AN INTERVIEW WITH GORE VIDAL

by Marc Cooper

H e might be America's last small-r republican. Gore Vidal, now seventy-six, has made a lifetime out of critiquing America's imperial impulses and has—through two dozen novels and hundreds of essays—argued tempestuously that the United States should retreat back to its more Jeffersonian roots, that it should stop meddling in the affairs of other nations and the private affairs of its own citizens.

That's the thread that runs through Vidal's latest bestseller—an oddly packaged collection of essays published in the wake of September 11 titled *Perpetual War for Perpetual Peace: How We Got to Be So Hated*. To answer the question in his subtitle, Vidal posits that we have no right to scratch our heads over what motivated the perpetrators of the two biggest terror attacks in our history: the 1995 Oklahoma City bombing and last September's twin-tower holocaust.

Vidal writes: "It is a law of physics (still on the books when last I looked) that in nature there is no action without reaction. The same appears to be true in human nature—that is, history." The "action" Vidal refers to is the hubris of an American empire abroad (illustrated by a twenty-page chart of two hundred U.S. overseas military adventures since the end of World War II) and a budding police state at home. The inevitable "reaction," says Vidal, is nothing less than the bloody handiwork of Osama bin Laden and Timothy McVeigh. "Each was enraged," he says, "by our government's reckless assaults upon other societies" and was, therefore, "provoked" into answering with horrendous violence.

Some might take that to be a suggestion that America had it coming on September 11. So when I met up with Vidal in the Hollywood Hills home he maintains (while still residing most of his time in Italy), the first question I asked him was this:

Marc Cooper: Are you arguing that the three thousand civilians killed on September 11 somehow deserved their fate?

Gore Vidal: I don't think we, the American people, deserved what happened. Nor do we deserve the sort of governments we have had over the last forty years. Our governments have brought this upon us by their actions all over the world. I have a list in my new book that gives the reader some idea how busy we have been. Unfortunately, we get only disinformation from the *New York Times* and other official places. Americans have no idea of the extent of their government's mischief. The number of military strikes we have made unprovoked, against other countries, since 1947–48 is more than 250. These are major strikes everywhere from Panama to Iran. And it isn't even a complete list. It doesn't include places like Chile, as that was a CIA operation. I was listing only military attacks.

Americans are either not told about these things or are told we attacked them because . . . well . . . Noriega is the center of all world drug traffic and we have to get rid of him. So we kill some Panamanians in the process. Actually we killed quite a few. And we brought in our air force. Panama didn't have an air force. But it looked good to have our air force there, busy, blowing up buildings. Then we kidnap their leader, Noriega, a former CIA man who worked loyally for the United States. We arrest him. Try him in an American court that has no jurisdiction over him and lock him up—nobody knows why. And that was supposed to end the drug trade because he had been demonized by the *New York Times* and the rest of the imperial press.

[The government] plays off [Americans'] relative innocence, or ignorance to be more precise. This is probably why geography has not really been taught since World War II—to keep people in the dark as to where we are blowing things up. Because Enron wants to blow them up. Or Unocal, the great pipeline company, wants a war going some place.

And people in the countries who are recipients of our bombs get angry. The Afghans had nothing to do with what happened to our country on September 11. But Saudi Arabia did. It seems like Osama is involved, but we don't really know. I mean, when we went into Afghanistan to take over the place and blow it up, our commanding general was asked how long it was going to take to find Osama bin Laden. And the commanding general looked rather surprised and said, "Well, that's not why we are here."

Oh no? So what was all this about? It was about the Taliban being very, very bad people and that they treated women very badly, you see. They're not really into women's rights, and we here are very strong on women's rights; and we should be with Bush on that one because he's taking those burlap sacks off of women's heads. Well, that's not what it was about.

What it was really about—and you won't get this any-where at the moment—is that this is an imperial grab for energy resources. Until now, the Persian Gulf has been our main source for imported oil. We went there, to Afghanistan, not to get Osama and wreak our vengeance. We went to Afghanistan partly because the Taliban—whom we had installed at the time of the Russian occupation—were getting too flaky and because Unocal, the California corporation, had made a deal with the Taliban for a pipeline to get the Caspian-area oil, which is the richest oil reserve on earth. They wanted to get that oil by pipeline through Afghanistan to Pakistan to Karachi and from there to ship it off to China, which would be enormously prof-itable. Whichever big company could cash in would make a fortune. And you'll see that all these companies go back to Bush or Cheney or to Rumsfeld or someone else on the gas-and-oil junta, which, along with the Pentagon, governs the United States.

We had planned to occupy Afghanistan in October, and Osama, or whoever it was who hit us in September, launched a preemptive strike. They knew we were coming. And this was a warning to throw us off guard.

With that background, it now becomes explicable why the first thing Bush did after we were hit was to get Senator Daschle and beg him not to hold an investigation of the sort any normal country would have done. When Pearl Harbor was struck, within twenty minutes the Senate and the House had a joint committee ready. Roosevelt beat them to it because he knew why we had been hit, so he set up his own committee. But none of this was to come out, and it hasn't come out.

Marc Cooper: Still, even if one reads the chart of military interventions in your book and concludes that, indeed, the U.S. government is a "source of evil"—to lift a phrase—can't you conceive that there might be other forces of evil as well? Can't you imagine forces of religious obscurantism, for example, that act independently of us and might do bad things to us, just because they are also evil?

Gore Vidal: Oh, yes. But you picked the wrong group. You picked one of the richest families in the world—the bin Ladens. They are extremely close to the royal family of Saudi Arabia, which has conned us into acting as their bodyguard against their own people—who are even more fundamentalist than they are. So we are dealing with a powerful entity if it is Osama.

What isn't true is that people like him just come out of the blue. You know, the average American thinks we just give away billions in foreign aid, when we are the lowest in foreign aid among developed countries. And most of what we give goes to Israel and a little bit to Egypt.

I was in Guatemala when the CIA was preparing its attack on the Arbenz government [in 1954]. Arbenz, who was a democratically elected president, mildly socialist. His state had no revenues; its biggest income maker was United Fruit Company. So Arbenz put the tiniest of taxes on bananas, and Henry Cabot Lodge got up in the Senate and said the Communists have taken over Guatemala and we must act. He got to Eisenhower, who sent in the CIA, and they overthrew the government. We installed a military dictator, and there's been nothing but bloodshed ever since.

Now, if I were a Guatemalan and I had the means to drop something on somebody in Washington, or anywhere Americans were, I would be tempted to do it. Especially if I had lost my entire family and seen my country blown to bits because United Fruit didn't want to pay taxes. Now, that's the way we operate. And that's why we got to be so hated.

Marc Cooper: You've spent decades bemoaning the erosion of civil liberties and the conversion of the U.S. from a republic into what you call an empire. Have the aftereffects of September 11, things like the USA Patriot Bill, merely pushed us further down the road or are they, in fact, some sort of historic turning point?

Gore Vidal: The second law of thermodynamics always rules: Everything is always running down. And so is our Bill of Rights. The current junta in charge of our affairs, one not legally elected, but put in charge of us by the Supreme Court in the interests of the oil and gas and defense lobbies, have used first Oklahoma City and now September 11 to further erode things.

And when it comes to Oklahoma City and Tim McVeigh, well, he had his reasons as well to carry out his dirty deed. Millions of Americans agree with his general reasoning, though no one, I think, agrees with the value of blowing up children. But the American people, yes, they instinctively know when the government goes off the rails like it did at Waco and Ruby Ridge. No one has been elected president in the last fifty years unless he ran against the federal government. So the government should get through its head that it is hated not only by foreigners whose countries we have wrecked, but also by Americans whose lives have been wrecked.

The whole Patriot movement in the U.S. was based on folks run off their family farms. Or had their parents or grandparents run off. We have millions of disaffected

American citizens who do not like the way the place is run and see no place in it where they can prosper. They can be slaves. Or pick cotton. Or whatever the latest uncomfortable thing there is to do. But they are not going to have, as Richard Nixon said, "a piece of the action."

Marc Cooper: And yet Americans seem quite susceptible to a sort of jingoistic "enemy-of-the-month club" coming out of Washington. You say millions of Americans hate the federal government. But something like 75 percent of Americans say they support George W. Bush, especially on the issue of the war.

Gore Vidal: I hope you don't believe those figures. Don't you know how the polls are rigged? It's simple. After 9/11 the country was really shocked and terrified. [Bush] does a little war dance and talks about evil axis and all the countries he's going to go after. And how long it is all going to take, he says with a happy smile, because it means billions and trillions for the Pentagon and for his oil friends. And it means curtailing our liberties, so this is all very thrilling for him. He's right out there reacting, bombing Afghanistan. Well, he might as well have been bombing Denmark. Denmark had nothing to do with 9/11. And neither did Afghanistan—at least, the Afghanis didn't.

So the question is still asked, are you standing tall with the president? Are you standing with him as he defends us?

Eventually, they will figure it out.

Marc Cooper: They being who? The American people?

Gore Vidal: Yeah, the American people. They are asked these quick questions. Do you approve of him? Oh yeah, yeah, yeah. Oh yeah, he blew up all those funny-sounding cities over there.

That doesn't mean they like him. Mark my words. He will leave office the most unpopular president in history. The junta has done too much wreckage.

They were suspiciously very ready with the Patriot Act as soon as we were hit. Ready to lift habeas corpus, due process, the attorney-client privilege. They were ready. Which means they have already got their police state. Just take a plane anywhere today, and you are in the hands of an arbitrary police state.

Marc Cooper: Don't you want to have that kind of protection when you fly?

Gore Vidal: It's one thing to be careful, and we certainly want airplanes to be careful against terrorist attacks. But this is joy for them, for the federal government. Now they've got everybody because everybody flies.

Marc Cooper: Let's pick away at one of your favorite bones, the American media. Some say they have done a better-than-usual job since 9/11. But I suspect you're not buying that?

Gore Vidal: No, I don't buy it. Part of the year, I live in Italy. And I find out more about what's going on in the Middle East by reading the British, the French, even the Italian press. Everything here is slanted. I mean, to watch Bush doing his little war dance in Congress . . . about "evil-doers" and this "axis of evil"—Iran, Iraq and North Korea. I thought, he doesn't even know what the word "axis" means. Somebody just gave it to him. And the press didn't even call him on it. This is about as mindless a statement as you could make. Then he comes up with about a dozen other countries that might have "evil people" in them, who might commit "terrorist acts." What is a terrorist act? Whatever he thinks is a terrorist act. And we are going to go after them. Because we are good and they are evil. And we're "gonna git 'em."

Anybody who could get up and make that speech to the American people is not himself an idiot, but he's convinced we are idiots. And we are not idiots. We are cowed.

Cowed by disinformation from the media, a skewed view of the world, and atrocious taxes that subsidize this permanent war machine. And we have no representation. Only the corporations are represented in Congress. That's why only 24 percent of the American people cast a vote for George W. Bush.

Marc Cooper: I know you'd hate to take this to the ad hominem level, but indulge me for a moment. What about George W. Bush, the man?

Gore Vidal: You mean George W. Bush, the cheerleader. That's the only thing he ever did of some note in his life. He had some involvement with a baseball team . . .

Marc Cooper: He owned it . . .

Gore Vidal: Yeah, he owned it, bought with other people's money. Oil people's money. So he's never really worked, and he shows very little capacity for learning. For them to put him up as president and for the Supreme Court to make sure that he won was as insulting as when his father, George Bush, appointed Clarence Thomas to the Supreme Court—done just to taunt the liberals. And then, when he picked Quayle for his vice president, that showed such contempt for the American people. This was someone as clearly unqualified as Bush Sr. was to be president. Because Bush Sr., as Richard Nixon said to a friend of mine when Bush was elected [*imitating Nixon*], "He's a lightweight, a complete lightweight, there's nothing there. He's a sort of person you appoint to things."

So the contempt for the American people has been made more vivid by the two Bushes than all of the presidents before them. Although many of them had the same contempt. But they were more clever about concealing it.

Marc Cooper: Should the U.S. just pack up its military from everywhere and go home?

Gore Vidal: Yes. With no exceptions. We are not the world's policeman. And we cannot even police the United States, except to steal money from the people and generally wreak havoc. The police are perceived quite often, and correctly, in most parts of the country as the enemy. I think it is time we roll back the empire—it is doing no one any good. It has cost us trillions of dollars, which makes me feel it's going to fold on its own because there isn't going to be enough money left to run it.

Marc Cooper: You call yourself one of the last defenders of the American Republic against the American Empire. Do you have any allies left? I mean, we really don't have a credible opposition in this country, do we?

Gore Vidal: I sometimes feel like I am the last defender of the republic. There are plenty of legal minds who defend the Bill of Rights, but they don't seem very vigorous. I mean, after 9/11 there was silence as one after another of these draconian, really totalitarian laws were put in place.

Marc Cooper: So what's the way out of this? Back in the '80s, you used to call for a new sort of populist constitutional convention. Do you still believe that's the fix?

Gore Vidal: Well, it's the least bloody. Because there will be trouble, and big trouble. The loons got together to get a balanced-budget amendment, and they got a majority of states to agree to a constitutional convention. Senator Sam Ervin, now dead, researched what would happen in such a convention, and apparently everything would be up for grabs. Once we the people are assembled, as the Constitution requires, we can do anything. We can throw out the whole executive, the judiciary, the Congress. We can put in a Tibetan lama. Or turn the country into one big Scientological clearing center.

And the liberals, of course, are the slowest and the stupidest, because they do not understand their interests. The right wing are the bad guys, but they know what they want—everybody else's money. And they know they don't like blacks and they don't like minorities. And they like to screw everyone along the way.

But once you know what you want, you are in a stronger position than those who can only say, "Oh no, you mustn't do *that*." That we must have free speech. Free speech for what? To agree with the *New York Times*?

The liberals always say, "Oh my, if there is a constitutional convention, they will take away the Bill of Rights." But they have already done it! It is gone. Hardly any of it is left. So if they, the famous "they," would prove to be a majority of the American people and did not want a Bill of Rights, then I say, "Let's just get it over with. Let's just throw it out the window. If you don't want it, you won't have it."